THE SPIRITUAL LIFE OF THE PRIEST

The Spiritual Life
of the Priest

BY

FATHER M. EUGENE BOYLAN, O.C.R.,

Author of *This Tremendous Lover*
and *Difficulties in Mental Prayer*

THE NEWMAN PRESS
WESTMINSTER, MARYLAND
1949

Nihil Obstat : Jacobus P. Bastible
Censor Deputatus

Imprimatur : Daniel
Episcopus Corcagiensis
13 Julii, 1949

Cum Permissu Superiorum

To Mary

the Mother of Christ

and

Mediatrx of All Graces

INTRODUCTION

This book contains a collection of articles which were written for the American monthly *The Priest*. Their style, structure, and general treatment were dictated by that circumstance. At first, it was thought that a more fundamental treatment could be introduced when the articles were being printed in book-form, but it was soon seen that a complete recasting of the whole would be necessary. So it was decided to leave fundamentals for future treatment and to print the articles in their original form.

There are accordingly some notable omissions. For example, there is little or no reference to the Holy Ghost, who should play so great a part in the life of the priest ; there is no attempt to examine a priest's obligation to seek perfection nor to indicate his hopes of reaching a high degree of prayer ; the treatment of humility is confined to one chapter, although we believe it to be the essential foundation of all spiritual life and work. However, we hope that what is here may prove helpful to diocesan priests, whose vocation we consider to be one of the most difficult of all.

Readers on this side of the Atlantic will please note that these pages were written with American conditions in view, and that in accordance with the request of American editors, we have written freely and unreservedly. Our intention is not to criticize but to be helpful and encouraging. There are many shortcomings in what we have written, but we hope that those very shortcomings will inspire more competent pens to give a fuller and more satisfactory work.

We would have liked to have further elaborated the fundamental place of the Mass in a priest's life, but the present format did not allow of it. May Mary the Mother of the Whole Christ use these pages to bring us all closer to Her Son, our High Priest and Victim !

Mount St. Joseph Abbey,
    Roscrea, Ireland.
    2nd February, 1949.

CONTENTS

"I HAVE CALLED YOU FRIENDS. . . ."

IT IS FAIRLY SAFE to say that we priests can all remember a time in our early days when we made up our minds that we were going to be good men and good priests. We may, perhaps, when forming that purpose, have stressed zeal in the ministry rather than personal holiness, but at least we decided that our spiritual life would not be neglected; we resolved never to give up mental prayer or spiritual reading, and we chose certain other practices to which we intended to be faithful. We were going to preach the Gospel; yes—but we were going to be sincere about it, and to practise what we preached. It is fairly safe, too, to say that few of us can look back on those good intentions without realizing that things now are not quite what we intended or hoped they would be. Somehow—for one reason or another—they did not work out just that way. A time came when we felt that the plans and the habits formed in the seminary did not quite fit in with life in a parish. The things that used to move us lost their appeal. The fervour that we anticipated in handling the Blessed Sacrament did not last. Hearing confessions became weary work, and the thrill of giving absolution soon disappeared. Prayer—well, the less said about that the better. We still have our office to "say", and, thank God, we still "say" it; but much of its significance has faded. We try to finish it quickly, so as to have time to say a few "real prayers", and even there, our old favourites have let us down; they no longer seem to have their former meaning. Perhaps things have even gone further. Some of us may have decided that, after all, holiness is not the main thing. There is plenty of work to be done in the parish, and the great thing is to do it; holiness is not for men like us. So we come to a sort of a compromise with ourselves. Every time a book or a remark seems likely to reproach us, we are quick to use our ministry as a lightning conductor to pass the stroke to someone else; we immediately decide how perfectly that would apply to so-and-so, or how useful it would be for such-and-such a sermon. We even build up some new chapters in theology to justify our position—a really "practical" theology. We become adepts at finding some in the diocese who do *this*, and others who do *that*—and we go and do likewise; combining in ourselves the "customs" of the whole diocese in so far as suits our particular desires. After all, why should a man desire in any way to vary from a kindly race of men? Is not custom the best interpreter of the law? And so on. Each of us can fill in many chapters in the story for himself.

If we are honest with ourselves, we will feel that somewhere or other we made a mistake or took a wrong turning, though perhaps we cannot tell exactly where. Perhaps we tried too much at the start; perhaps we had a wrong notion of what God wanted from us; perhaps we were frightened at the thought of the endless renunciation that faithful friendship with Him seemed to involve. Perhaps, indeed, we misunderstood His handling of our case, and, just when He began to advance us in holiness by undoing some of our work as a preliminary to substituting some of His own, we decided that we had better cut our losses and be satisfied to be like the rest of men. Perhaps . . . well—there are many possibilities, and there is no need to enumerate them all. Each one of us will have to diagnose his own case. With a view to aiding him to treat it, we shall try to draw up what a medical student once called a "gunshot prescription"—he did not know what was wrong with the patient, so he put in a little of everything to make sure of hitting the mark. And so in this book we shall try to cover the main points of the spiritual life of the priest, in a practical way. Each one, with the help of God, may thus find out whether anything is wrong in his own case and decide what must be done to to put things right. But there are two things upon which we must all be agreed. First, no matter how far or how badly things have gone wrong—even if we are completely off the rails—God *can* put all right, and, what is more, He is ready to do so. He is our Saviour, and it is precisely because we are men—sinful men—who have gone astray, that we have a claim upon His help as our Saviour. He is God; therefore there is no limit to His power or to His mercy in helping us; He can even turn our failings to good account. On this first point we must be certain. For if we do not trust God as our Saviour, we shall not have the courage to be honest with ourselves and to admit our failings and infirmities. Each of us has to learn to imitate St. Paul and glory in his infirmities precisely in order that the power of Christ may dwell in him. Secondly, we must agree to take Our Lord at His word. He said that His yoke is easy and His burden light. If we let our imagination frighten us with pictures of the impossible demands of penance and self-abnegation that His friendship is going to make upon us, can we really say that we believe what He said? Actually, when He does ask us to give up something, it is only in order that He may give us something else instead, which is a hundred times better. We have His word for that, too, and surely we can take God at His word!

Having agreed upon these two points, let us now consider the practical aspect of the spiritual life. On this point we may not agree. Many consider that a practical discussion of a priest's life should give a detailed programme for the day and a direct solution of all its difficulties. Some programme is necessary, indeed, but perhaps there is a better way of leading up to it which, in the long run, is more practical. Nearly all programmes, sooner or later, have to yield to circumstances. They are either too rigid, and they break under the strain, or else they are too elastic, and they stretch and yield—*ad infinitum*. For a priest, who has to lead a full spiritual life under the most varying circumstances, it would seem that the more practical and the more effective thing would be to form an *attitude*, rather than a programme. If that attitude is correct and sincere, and has its roots in a man's heart and in his convictions, he should not have over-much difficulty in planning his own spiritual life with the help of a competent adviser, and in adapting his plan, without destroying it, to each set of circumstances. At any rate we can see how far we can get by working on those lines. What, then, must be the attitude of the priest? The best answer is that indicated by Our Lord to His Apostles at the Last Supper. He laid down the cardinal principle of the spiritual life and the foundation of all spiritual fruitfulness, when He said: "*Abide in Me, and I in you. As the branch cannot bear fruit of itself unless it abide in the vine, so neither can you unless you abide in Me. I am the Vine: you are the branches: he that abideth in Me and I in him, the same beareth much fruit, for without Me you can do nothing,*" (John xv, 45). That one phrase of Our Lord's: "*Abide in Me,*" sums up everything, and it will re-echo frequently in these pages. But before we examine its full implication, let us consider a special aspect of the relationship of the priest to Our Lord which is shown in the same discourse when Our Lord said: "*I will not now call you servants . . . but I have called you friends*," (John xv, 15).

Here is the first answer to our question. The priest must be *the friend of Jesus*. He is more than a mere servant, and so he must offer Jesus something more than mere service—for He wants more than that. This is a point we need to realise: no matter what may be our success in the harvest-field, no matter how much fruit we have gathered for Him, He will not be content with that alone. In fact, He has no need of our services. He has many other instruments that He could use for His work if He so wished. But although He appoints priests for the good of souls, His choice of *you* and *me* to be priests arises from His desire to make *us* His friends for all eternity. For that reason alone He has done us the honour of choosing us to work in partnership with Him. Consequently, no matter what fruit we gather for Him—and be it noted in passing, there is a great difference between gathering fruit and bringing forth fruit—if we do not give Him our friendship, we fail Him, we let Him down.

Let us now go back to St. John's Gospel and read the words of Jesus with a new accent: "I have chosen *you*: and have appointed *you*, that *you* should go, and should bring forth fruit; and *your* fruit should remain: that whatsoever *you* shall ask of the Father in My name, He may give it to *you*," (John xv, 16). In other words, Reverend Father, Our Lord has chosen *you* to do something which He could do ever so much better Himself—*per se vel per alium*—because He wants *you* to have the benefit of it, and because He wants *you* for His special friend. Perhaps that may throw some light on the inadequacy of our spiritual outlook and practice. *The Imitation of Christ* gives utterance to Our Lord's sentiments: "*Whatsoever thou givest besides thyself, I regard not; for I seek not thy gift, but thyself. As it would not suffice thee, if thou hadst all things but Me; so neither can it please Me whatsoever thou givest, as long as thou offerest not thyself*," (Book iv, c.8). No one else can give Him *our* friendship or *our* love. It is the one thing in our lives that is irreplaceable; all the rest could be done by somebody else. Our first step then towards

forming a correct attitude is to remember that Jesus made
each of us a priest because He wants each of us for a friend.
Pius X in his *Letter to Priests*[1] quotes the text, "I have called
you friends," and adds: "*We priests, Christ's representatives,
must bear Him in ourselves; and as His ambassadors, where He
wills, there we must be. Since the sure and only sign of true friendship
is to will the same thing*—idem velle, idem nolle; *we must let
that mind be in us which was in Christ Jesus, 'holy, innocent, and
undefiled.' As His ambassadors then, we must win men to belief in
His law and teaching by first observing them ourselves, for it behoves
us, who, as sharing His power, lift up men from the bondage of sin,
to strive with all possible care not to be ourselves ensnared.*"
(Pius X: *Haerent Animo*, Aug. 4th, 1908). This particular
Encyclical is full of very helpful passages and we
earnestly beg all our readers to study it. For the
moment we take from it three points: first, that a priest is
the friend of Jesus whom he must bear in himself; secondly,
that a priest shares in the power of Jesus; and thirdly—let us
sum it up in the pregnant phrases—"*idem velle, idem nolle.*"
These three points will suffice for the moment. There is
little use in considering the usual reasons upon which our
need of holiness is based. We have heard them so often that
they have either taken their effect by now, or else we have
become well inoculated against them. But there is one thing
we should all remember. It is very easy for us to be mistaken
about our part in the fruitfulness of our ministry. Every
single step that any soul takes towards God is primarily and
essentially the work of grace, and the person who brings
down that grace is the person who gets most merit for the
advance of the soul. It is true that we priests are *ex officio*
ministers of grace; that is, we can always call upon the results
of someone else's "prayer and fasting." Our Lord and His
Mother have done their share—it is more than a share—in
obtaining every single grace we "minister"; but there are
others, too, who "fill up what is wanting of the sufferings of
Christ for His Church." It is these "others"—this "someone"
—who will get most of the credit for our ministry unless we
too become power houses of grace instead of mere trans-
mission lines. Our Lord warned us, "*unless you abide in
Me. . . .*" No long consideration, then, should be necessary

[1] English translation published by B.O.W. in 1918.

to see that we have to build up a living image of Jesus Christ in our minds, and to keep that image fresh and effective in our lives. To that we must join a conviction of our complete dependence upon Him in every action of our priesthood, and we must develop a generous desire to return His friendship. The first step to this end lies in the daily use of three things which are very closely connected, reading, reflection, and private prayer.

These three we shall examine briefly in the following chapters, leaving their fuller treatment for a later stage. But before we go any further, let us rid ourselves of all vain fears. God will not ask us for anything unreasonable. He knows the clay we are made of, and He knows just what we have made of ourselves. We must always remember that He never asks us to do anything for Him without, at the same time, coming to be our partner in doing it; for He is our full Supplement and our perfect Complement in all things. It does not matter what we are; He can sanctify us, if we are but willing. Even as simple Christians we have Him dwelling in our souls to sanctify us; but as priests, we are sharers in His sanctifying power for our own sanctification as well as for that of others. Since we are bound to sanctify ourselves as priests, we can count upon Him for all the graces and help necessary even for the heights of holiness. Even if we feel we are hardened sinners, we must not forget that "*This man receiveth sinners.*" That was His characteristic in the eyes of the Jews. Let us have no doubt about it; He will certainly receive you and me.

SPIRITUAL READING

SINCE OUR LIVES as Christians and our fruitfulness as priests have their root in our abiding in Christ, our first aim must be to provide for the maintenance and the growth of that union. The Sacraments, of course, have their part to play in the process, but first let us consider those three important exercises previously mentioned, which we must perform in order to promote this growth: reading, reflection and prayer. In the time table of every seminary and religious house, there is a place for an exercise called meditation or mental prayer. This exercise is generally assumed to consist in the methodical consideration of a previously prepared subject, which has been divided up into "points"; and in this way one is led to the production of a number of acts or "affections," often called a colloquy, as well as to the formation of some practical resolution for one's conduct. The principle underlying the exercise is, from the practical point of view, one of the most important in the whole spiritual life. It amounts roughly to this, that a man must daily think of God and of his own relations with Him, and that he must also daily talk to God, both of God and of himself, and of their relations with one another. The manner in which this principle is realized is capable of much variation and, to our mind, should be freely adapted to suit individual needs if the practice is to be kept up during one's life as a priest. There is no need to discuss here the details of the methods usually proposed for meditation. There are many books on the subject, and most priests have a fair practical experience of the exercise. Some have found a method which works quite well and is a great help to them, but many of us have found that the whole thing has become wearisome and apparently futile, and have given it up as a useless burden. The possible reasons for that failure are manifold, and in the hope of helping people who have got into that position we have endeavoured elsewhere to suggest some ideas on the subject. As we can only treat the subject briefly here, we hope we shall be pardoned for referring the reader to that book for a fuller treatment of the question, (cf. Boylan: *Difficulties in Mental Prayer*.)

It would seem that three different things have been telescoped into this one exercise of "meditation"; reading,
reflection, and true prayer. Each of these has an important
place in the spiritual life, and we propose to examine each
one, and then to make provision for them all in two set
exercises, namely, spiritual reading, and private prayer, with
a third informal practice: reflection. One reason why so
many fail at mental prayer is that they are trying to make a
fire without fuel—they have given up regular spiritual
reading. Apart from the Sacraments, such reading, in its
own way, is the first essential of a priest's spiritual life.

There is no use in arguing about it. You are going to be
asked to give an hour daily to the combination of these three
exercises, no matter how busy you are. No man is too busy
to eat. Neither is any man too busy to feed his soul. And
if we starve our souls, we shall deprive our ministry—busy
though it be—of its fruitfulness. In defence of this demand,
we promise you that we shall cheerfully take full responsibility
at the Judgment Seat of God for any loss to souls, or to your
work as a priest, that might be occasioned by devoting an
hour daily to these exercises, even though your attempts
seem to be fruitless as far as devotion is concerned. There
are two purposes in spiritual reading. One is to educate
ourselves about God—especially about God Incarnate—and
about the spiritual life. The other is to keep our ideas of
God and of the spiritual life fresh in our minds and to make
them influence our actions. In regard to the first, we must
make ourselves well acquainted with the Person of Our Lord,
with His history and His habits, His views and His tastes;
for we are to live as His friends. The Gospels and some of
the various lives of Our Lord (e.g. that by Archbishop
Goodier), must be often in our hands, not to acquire a mere
academic knowledge or to obtain matter for our sermons—
that must never be the primary object of our spiritual
reading or of our meditation—but in order to make us live
as the friends of Jesus. Since we are to share in His power,
we should build up a good knowledge of grace and its
working, and of our place in the Mystical Body of Christ;
and become, in addition, well acquainted with the principles
of the spiritual life, especially in regard to the life of prayer.
If we do not become men with an interior life, we cannot

abide in the Vine and we shall not bring forth much fruit.

As to what books to read: that is a personal matter. In building up a picture of Our Lord, each will have to follow his own taste in books. In regard to the spiritual life, however, we venture to make a few tentative suggestions. As we are not familiar with the many excellent works published in the United States, we have to confine our titles to those which we ourselves have read.

The Spiritual Life by Tanquerey should be on the shelves of every priest as an incomparable book of reference. Despite its length, every priest should read it through at least once. But to commence one's study of the spiritual life we would suggest *Spiritual Instruction* by Abbot Blosius. Although we do not like to cry the wares of our own Order, we cannot help drawing attention to *The Soul of the Apostolate* by Dom Chautard, O.C.R., as a book which every priest should read. The works of Fr. Kearney, C.S.Sp., have also been found most helpful, and of them we suggest *My Spiritual Exercises* as a very practical guide. There are two excellent works on prayer: *The Degrees of the Spiritual Life* by Canon Saudreau, and *The Ways of Mental Prayer* by Dom Lehodey, O.C.R. Those who are beset by aridity at prayer will find much help in *On Prayer* by De Caussade, S.J., and *The Science of Prayer* by De Besse, O.F.M. Cap. There are few books better than *Acquired Contemplation* by Fr. Gabriel of St. Mary Magdalen O.D.C.: it appears in a volume under the title: *St. John of the Cross—Doctor of Contemplation and Divine Love.* This gives in a short form an account of "post-meditation" developments, and discusses what the ordinary soul may hope to achieve with good-will.

For an insight into the Mass, it is hard to improve on Dom Vonier, O.S.B., *A Key to the Doctrine of the Eucharist.* A little book by De Jaegher, S.J., *One With Jesus,* is an invaluable account of the indwelling of God in our souls. Finally, we insist that a priest's reading *must* include some literature on Our Lady. If we might select one of a number of excellent books, it would be *The Mother of Divine Grace* by Le Rohellec, C.S.Sp. Those who wish to make devotion to Our Lady the foundation of their spiritual life should read *The De Montfort Way.* These are but a few suggestions; other titles will be given in the context of these articles.

Once the initial work of our education has been done, our further aim in spiritual reading should be rather to recall than to acquire knowledge, to deepen what we already know, to form convictions that will influence our life, and so to ensure that the motives by which we live and act are super-natural. In fact, our reading is going to be a sort of informal meditation in the strict sense of the name, and those meditation books which carry a personal appeal are the very thing that can be recommended for such reading. But whatever our book may be, we should read it somewhat in the same way as one would read an insurance policy or a contract, or a catalogue or a specification for a new car—that is, *with careful consideration.*

Reading of this type should be commenced with a short but very sincere prayer. It is hard to improve on: "Speak, Lord, Thy servant heareth," and having commenced thus, we should try to read with a spirit of faith. We have to be ready to hear the voice of God speaking to us—not to our congregation or to the "other fellow"—between the lines, and we must be prepared to stop and listen to Him, to think over what He has said, and to give Him what He requests. This is where the fault in our meditation lies: we do not want to be asked for certain things, and that is often the reason why we hurry on, or why our conversations with God run dry. We do not want to listen because of the possibility of unwelcome demands being made upon our friendship; then He decides to refrain from proposing to us something whose refusal would only increase the gap between us and Him; and so there is an awkward silence or a sudden rush of activity. This, of course, is more likely to happen in prayer, but it can happen even in reading. It is but one of the many possible examples of the inter-dependence of the different parts and exercises of the spiritual life. Progress in any one leads to progress in all, and defects in one can interfere with many others. In reading, this willingness to hear God speaking is of capital importance. We should try to do our reading in His presence, just as a child plays in the "presence" of its mother sitting in the background. But this means a fairly clear conscience and the absence of a deliberate determination to keep something back from God. Such a determination is not to be confused with the feeling of difficulty or distaste we may experience towards certain things He might want. He is not offended by that; all He wants is that we should ask Him to give us grace to be generous in overcoming that difficulty. In this, as in everything, He is always our *Saviour*.

Another source of difficulty in spiritual reading is the style in which many books are written. Quite a number of the best books on the spiritual life are translations from a foreign language, which carry with them an air of affected piety that seems somewhat artificial. When to the difference of language of origin there is added the difference of time in origin, the effect of unreality may be increased. Social conventions differ considerably in various nations and generations, and both outward deportment and literary expressions are, to a certain extent, matters of convention. What many writers on the European continent—especially those of an earlier century—would consider to be the normal expression of christian charity, may seem to English-speaking people of today to be, if not hypocrisy, at least exaggerated affectation. This is but an example; there are many other external things that belong to their time and place of origin, and without considering them in detail we can admit that a certain reserve must be used about accepting what one reads. Not everything that is written applies to each individual case. There are even different schools of spirituality, and the reader will have to set aside what does not fit in with the present stage of his own spiritual development. Each stage has its particular needs and its particular limitations, and until a fire is burning well, one must be careful not to kill it by putting on too much fuel. Prudence is always essential. Books alone, therefore, are not quite sufficient; one needs an occasional talk with a wise and understanding counsellor, but that point must be left for later discussion.

One thing is very desirable. When reading does start a suitable train of thought, it is good to follow it up—putting down one's book, or even, say, going for a walk, if that is helpful. This is the informal reflection of which we spoke, and which we recommend as a habit that every priest should try to develop. The point to note is that such reflection should be referred to God's relationship with one's own self—not with one's parishioners or penitents; and be it noted, too, that we do not include under this type of reflection, "apologetic" thinking—that is, thinking out arguments for converts, etc. Such thought is necessary, but it does not supply for the omission of true "meditation" as a source of one's own spiritual life. One other point! If our reflection leads us to conclusions that seem particularly unpleasant or that make great demands on our courage, it would be well to postpone the application of such conclusions where there is room for reasonable doubt, and keep an open mind, until one has had an opportunity to talk the thing over with a "wise man." This may seem strange advice, as it may leave room for temporary self-deception. Its purpose, however, is to avoid the danger of saying "no" to God as a result of some exaggerated or mistaken idea of what He asks of us and so spoiling our intimate friendship with Him. The devil often tries to destroy our good will by exaggerating our notions of what we may have to do. It is important to be reasonable even with oneself and to remember that individual needs must be considered; otherwise, one develops a habit of evasion and does not look facts in the face.

This informal reflection can easily be changed into informal prayer by talking things over with Our Lord instead of with oneself. It can arise directly out of one's reading, and one should encourage such a development if it commences, for we must never forget that God is in the soul of every man in the state of grace, waiting for his friendship and companionship. In this connection it is important to realize that such prayer can be quite informal and conversational. It is true that God has a claim to our reverence and adoration, but that we give Him by the Mass and by the Office. At the moment He wants to be treated as our Father and our Friend. Ultimately we *must* treat Him as our Lover; and as St. Bernard says : "Love knows nothing of reverence." There is much more that could be said on reading and reflection, but as we want to show their effect upon mental prayer, we shall pass on to that subject in our next chapter. The essential thing is to read regularly; even ten minutes daily would be better than a few hours once a week. Reading can be an act of religion, and we know what value that can have; moreover, it makes mental prayer much easier, and enables us to do without those involved methods that many of us find so wearisome. If a priest wants to bear fruit, let him abide in Christ. If he wants to abide in Christ, let him seek Christ daily in his reading. That search will make it easier to find Him also in the Sacraments, in prayer, in humility, in one's neighbour and in doing the will of God.

TALKING WITH GOD

THE MORE A MAN reads and reflects, the more he can know *about* God; but all his reading and reflection notwithstanding, he will never know God Himself nor will he grow in that friendship which our Lord proposed to His priests, unless he converse with God frequently in prayer. This particular exercise of the spiritual life devoted to conversation with God is usually called either "mental prayer" or "meditation." These names are sanctioned by usage and authority—for Canon Law requires priests to devote themselves daily to "mental prayer"—and it is not easy to find an alternative name which would be an improvement. Yet both of these names have led to much misunderstanding, and caused unnecessary difficulty at prayer. The term "mental" prayer is taken by some to imply complete distinction from "vocal" prayer, and they decide therefore that words should never be used in its exercise; this is a capital error. In practice, vocal prayer indicates that form of prayer in which one makes use of set formulae of words, endeavouring, at the same time, with more or less success, to conform one's mind to their meaning. But if the mind and heart are not in some way at work, there is no true prayer at all. The Divine Office is an example of vocal prayer; so also is the recitation of the *Memorare*. By mental prayer we here understand that form of prayer in which one endeavours to originate the thought in one's own mind, and so to get the will to move in some way towards God. In practice, it makes no difference to the existence of "mental" prayer whether this interior action manifests itself in external words or not; if the prayer originates interiorly, it is for practical purposes mental prayer. In vocal prayer, we say something given to us from outside and we endeavour to "mean" what we say. In mental prayer we first endeavour to "mean" something; whether we then say it in a standard formula or in our own words—whether in fact we say it in words at all or not—does not matter. In short, mental prayer means talking to God "in one's own words" though one may use no words at all! The paradox arises from the fact that even between human friends who know one another very well, smiles and gestures can speak volumes; they are very much one's "own words." But when there is question of our Divine Friend, to Whom our very thoughts are open, our minds and hearts can speak directly; their acts are "our own words" in this case. When words are used in mental prayer, it is to help us to form acts rather than to convey our acts to God. Mental prayer, in practice, then, does not exclude the use of words, but it can dispense with them when expedient to do so.

The term "meditation" may mislead even more than the expression "mental prayer." Not everyone can start talking to God in his own words from the first moment of his prayer. Most of us have to think of something to say to Him, and while this thinking is quite properly called meditation, yet, as such, it is not prayer. It is true, however, that while thus "meditating" one's heart *may* be making silent and unperceived acts of love of God which might be called prayer; then the real mental prayer consists in those acts, and the "meditation" is only a preparation or a prelude to prayer—a means to an end. It is essential to realize this point; for there are many who consider reflection to be the important thing at mental prayer, and the "acts" or "affections" merely an accidental, or at most, an integral part of it. The contrary is rather the case: the acts are the real prayer and all the rest purely the means to an end. It is true that there are other fruits to be gathered from the exercise as it is generally described, but as we pointed out in the previous chapter, provision for these is made by spiritual reading and reflection at some other time of the day. For the moment we want to *pray*.

The need for consideration at prayer in order to produce such acts varies with the individual and with one's progress. In this connection, there is a generally recognized division of mental prayer into three classes: discursive prayer, affective prayer, and simplified prayer. These three classes are often considered to be characteristic of the three "ways" or stages of the spiritual life: the purgative, the illuminative, and the unitive way respectively. Yet the parallel between a way of prayer and a particular stage of the spiritual life, must not be taken too literally. The three "ways" of praying can be found at any stage of the spiritual life, and possibly even in the one prayer; they are not sharply divided or mutually exclusive. When considerations predominate at the time of prayer, we have discursive prayer. This prayer too, is sometimes called "meditation," thus adding to the confusion occasioned by that unfortunate word. It is a prayer in which one helps oneself to produce "acts" by the "discourse" of reason, that is by consideration of some particular point. The name is generally confined to that prayer in which such consideration predominates; the acts are few and take up but little time. If, however, the acts come fairly freely and often, so that there is no need for much consideration at the time of prayer, and if these acts or "affections" tend to predominate, we have "affective prayer." This is really praying in one's own words, just as many Catholics do after Holy Communion. At a later stage, as one's friendship with Our Lord deepens, conversation with Him becomes much simpler in expression. Few words then are necessary; one may be often repeated, often our love or our adoration is quite silent. Sometimes one does no more than kneel before God, sinful and sorrowful. Prayer of this type may be called simplified prayer; it is sometimes called the "prayer of simplicity," but as some authors use this expression to indicate a special type of infused prayer (to which it is somewhat akin), we prefer to avoid the term.

However, one usually has to begin with discursive prayer, and here the question of method immediately arises. To cut a long discussion short, let us say that each one should use just as much or just as little method as he finds helpful. There are books and books of "methodized" prayer, which are of great help to some, but to others only a hindrance, for prayer is an individual thing, and methods purely means towards an end. All we have to say about the choice is, that if one must err, *err on the side of simplicity*. We go to prayer to pray—to talk to God. The first step then is to make contact with Him. True, He is always there, but we must advert to His presence, which in practice rather means adverting to *His* advertence to *our* presence. This needs deliberate effort; it involves a definite *decision* to turn to Him, and a definite breaking of all other "contacts." Our ultimate success at prayer depends greatly upon this whole-

hearted turning to God at the beginning of our prayer.
Our first instinct should be to adore Him. Let us do this in
the *simplest possible words*—words that we have made *our own;*
no fine speeches, no rhetoric or oratory, no striving after
effect! "You are my God and I adore You." If we *mean*
that, it may be enough, for sincerity and simplicity must be
the keynotes of our conversation with God. If we wish to
add more—well and good, as long as we mean it. We are
now praying; whether we vary our words, or keep saying the
same ones, we are still praying. The next step depends on
ourselves. We may want to tell God we love Him, or we
may feel the need of telling Him how sorry we are for having
offended Him. Let us do as we are urged, simply, sincerely,
and slowly. No counting of words or acts! No attempt to
rush things, to get in a lot of aspirations! Shakespeare puts
the principle perfectly: *"Use all gently!"* As long as we can
say anything about these sentiments or "mean" anything
about them, we are praying, and there is no need to proceed
further until that prayer ceases. This is true mental prayer.

But unfortunately it comes to an end—sooner or later.
It is possible, indeed, that it may not start at all. In either
case we have to fall back on "discourse"—or consideration,
to help us to pray. For this we need some subject, the choice
of which is, again, a personal matter, and we can only offer
suggestions. A good book of meditations, Hamon's for
example, or *To the Priesthood with Jesus,* would supply us with
material. The Gospel of the Mass of the day, some part or
chapter in our spiritual reading, the mysteries of the Rosary,
the Stations of the Cross, are all valuable sources of matter
for prayer. A series of subjects like the Stations is often of
great help, or again one can note certain passages in one's
daily reading and come back to them for prayer next day.
Having selected our subject we must start to consider some
particular aspect of it—"the first point." Here one notes
the probable need for some previous preparation. Linking
up prayer with spiritual reading helps to avoid multiplying
books and one could use a meditation book for part of one's
spiritual reading. But the man who is faithful to his daily
reading has removed half the difficulties in the approach to
mental prayer. Meditation books generally divide the
subject into a number of points and suggest the line of

thought to be followed, the conclusions to be drawn, and the acts and resolutions that are to result from it. We can adopt this plan in so far as it is helpful. Some minds will be satisfied with deciding upon their subject, noting a few points for consideration and mobilizing some general material to assist the consideration. Experience will naturally help us to decide what way suits us best, but we should so arrange our choice that the incidents of Our Lord's Life and Death are frequent subjects of our prayer.

To return now to our prayer! When the preliminary acts are finished, we have to reflect upon our subject. It is here that the faithful practice of daily reading and informal reflection will help very much to lessen what is one of the most wearisome tasks of the spiritual life. For if we read frequently, we should not need to think long before acts form themselves. Our personal view is that once these acts come, consideration can be left aside till it is needed again to revive our conversation with God. Reflection is usually done more or less by talking to ourselves about our own subject. It is a very good plan to change this, and to make our consideration by talking to *Our Lord* about the matter. To facilitate this we would suggest that one adds to the opening acts of the prayer a *very short* spiritual communion, inviting our Lord to come into one's soul. Now it is very desirable that we receive Him in that mystery which is the subject of our prayer, and there need be nothing artificial about this. The mysteries of Our Lord's life have a quasi-eternal existence of their own, and they belong, in a sense, to all the members of His Mystical Body. The unity of that Body, in which we and He are one, defies space and time: we here and now, in the twentieth century, in whatever part of the world we live can be quite really *one* with our Lord in any incident of His life in Palestine during the beginning of the first century of the Christian era.

If, then, the subject of our prayer is some such incident, let us stand beside Him in that incident and talk to Him about it, and about ourselves. Suppose it is the scene where He weeps over Jerusalem. Let us ask him gently: "Am I also one of those for whom You weep? Have I forgotten the things that are to my peace? Does my eagerness for success, for comfort, for a good time, hurt Your Heart? Am I perhaps one of those who refuse to be gathered under Your wings? Am I as full of myself as all that?" And so on.

If our subject be something more abstract as, for example, trust—then let us talk to Him about it. "Did you have me in mind when You said to the Apostles: 'O you of little faith, why do you doubt?'—Do I trust You enough? Am I perhaps putting all my trust in myself? That sermon I preached on Sunday—it seemed quite a good piece of work, but now it strikes me that perhaps You are hurt because I gave You such a small part in it. Did You really mean me to take St. Paul at his word—and literally glory in my infirmities? Because if You did—well, I'm afraid I'm letting You down very badly—I rather glory in the power I have to do good in Your service, and I can't say that my motives are what they should be." Now, conversation is impossible if one person keeps talking all the time, so we must pause to see whether He has perhaps something to say to us. In the last example given above, we may possibly hear a gentle inquiry—"Is it really in *My* service that you are working—or is it for your own glory? Did you ever think of the price I had to pay in suffering—and My Mother, too—to obtain for you the grace of your priesthood? Where did your natural power to preach come from?" If we are willing to listen, we shall hear Him speak, especially if we we are also willing to *heed* His gentle reproaches.

Resolutions then form themselves almost automatically. However, if Our Lord does not move us in some particular way, we ourselves should be ready to take the initiative and form some specific resolution that is practical and sincere. This type of prayer is half way between Discursive Prayer and Affective Prayer. It presupposes fidelity to daily reading, and also a good will with a fairly clear conscience. In other words, it means that, although we are sinners, we are not so obstinate that we will refuse to give up a particular sin when God brings it to our notice. If, however, there is somewhere in the borderland of our consciousness a determination to persist in some path of error that we really know is opposed to God's will, then our prayer will not be so easy. From the very start there will be constraint. All the time, there will be determination to avoid letting our thoughts run on "dangerous" lines, and if conversation with Our Lord does commence, we will be careful to steer it clear of "dangerous" topics. In other words we will not be sincere; we will be afraid to look God in the face, afraid to catch His eye. That is one reason why there is so much difficulty in mental prayer. We find it hard to start talking to God, because we are afraid that He will ask us to do something that we are determined *not* to do. Ultimately that means that all hope of conversation with God has to be abandoned. That means also that there can be no question of true friendship with Our Lord, and here we come upon the very close connection between mental prayer and the spiritual life in general. This connection is our justification for devoting so much space to the topic. To get mental prayer right, the rest of the spiritual life must be put right, so that apart from its own intrinsic importance, mental prayer is a valuable clinical thermometer for the health of our soul.

Failure in prayer is often due to failure in one of the four "purities" which are necessary for familiar friendship with Jesus. These are: purity of conscience, purity of heart, purity of mind, purity of action. We shall have to examine these four points in the course of our discussions, but here it is only necessary to advert to the general effect on our prayer and our relation with God of habits of sin, of strong and inordinate attachments, of pre-occupation with thoughts of the things of this world, and of serious failure to make our deeds correspond to our principles and ideals. Friendship with God must be sincere. He is always our Saviour, and He will always receive and save sinners, provided they are willing to become His friends. But friendship has its obligations and demands a certain sincerity with God and with oneself. Leaving this point for further notice, we may point out that there are other causes which may interfere with our prayers. A determination to persist in methodical consideration when one really wants to "pray"—i.e. to make acts—will lead to failure. Difficulty also arises if one is not content with simple acts, repeated if necessary, or if one refuses to be content with silent prayer when that is possible. Trying to force oneself to make numerous or complicated acts will mean trouble. The opposite mistakes are also common, for many dispense themselves from reflection at prayer too easily.

Then, too, a time of aridity comes to all of us when not even a good thought seems possible. Here one must fall back on a grim, resolute decision never to give up devoting a fixed time to this "fruitless" attempt at prayer every day. Merely staying on one's knees and doing one's best to avoid being deliberately distracted is a prayer of great value in these circumstances, and we must be convinced that there is no better use to which the time can be put. It is sometimes helpful to recite some favourite prayer very slowly—the *Anima Christi*, or the Litany of the Blessed Mother—so that the words and phrases become "our own," but even this may fail. Then perhaps a book may help to keep our thoughts on God. If we use a book, we should pause frequently to— well, to pray if we can, if not, to kneel before God in faith and hope. But whatever happens we must be determined that we will not give up the daily attempt. It will bring down many graces on our flock, and on our own souls.

THE NECESSITY FOR MENTAL PRAYER

EVEN AT THE risk of wearying the reader by our insistence and by partial repetition, we cannot leave the subject of mental prayer without some further discussion. Perhaps it would be an exaggeration to say that the whole spiritual life hinges upon mental prayer, but it is at least true that there is no exercise which can have such an effect on the spiritual life and which is itself so affected by that life. It therefore forms an excellent test of one's spiritual progress. Hence our insistence. To sum up the view already stated, we may say that there are three things which each priest must *decide* to do every day. The first is to nourish his mind with thoughts about God by reading; the second is to develop and to digest such thoughts by reflection; the third is to speak to God in his own words and his own way by prayer, using those thoughts if necessary. These three exercises are often telescoped into one and called meditation. We suggest separating them again into three different exercises, namely: spiritual reading, "personal" prayer, and reflection, and conscientiously devoting an hour for all three taken together. The allocation of that hour depends upon one's personal needs and accomplishments, but twenty minutes should be a minimum for prayer. The reflection can be done rather informally—on a walk for example—but one must check up occasionally to see that it *is* done. Spiritual reading must have its appointed time, and must never be discarded. The time set aside for prayer—we may call it mental prayer—must also be fixed and must not be left to chance. The morning is often suggested as the most suitable time, but not everybody will find it so. For some, the evening is more congenial, especially if one has a chance of making one's prayer before the Blessed Sacrament. If the evening is chosen, there are two points which call for notice. The first is that it is much more likely that things will turn up to interfere with an evening prayer than a morning one (and may we stress the fact that "evening" does *not* mean just before going to bed!), so some rule must be made to provide for accidents. Two periods of prayer next day might do that. The other point is, that when mental prayer is left until evening, some short informal "contact" must be made with Our Lord in the morning before Mass.

The priest's whole life is to be lived in close partnership with Our Lord—we are branches of the Vine—and the remembrance of that contact needs to be renewed at the start of each day's work. If a priest fails to do this, he will find himself attacking most of the day's work single-handed, a policy which is fatal and sterile for him. *A priest cannot perform a single act of his ministry alone!* He is not merely another Christ—he is one with Christ. That union must characterize his Mass, his office, his work—his whole life as a priest. Nowhere can it be better developed and made real than in mental prayer and in one's thanksgiving. Consequently even a short five minutes *praying*, as distinct from saying prayers, will make a great difference to the Mass and the breviary.

If proper provision is made for that morning meeting with our Divine Partner, there can be little objection to choosing whatever time of the day suits best for our prayer. In the last chapter we gave an example of how to start to pray, and we pointed out that facility in talking to Our Lord, or even in remaining silent in His presence was partly dependent upon the state of our spiritual life. However, not everyone will find it easy to pray as we suggested, and even fervent priests may find it extremely difficult to converse with God for any length of time. For such as these, there are other ways of praying. The slow, deliberate recital of a favourite prayer, with plenty of pauses, will help in some cases, and one should try to make the words of the prayer one's own by dwelling on them. The Psalms offer excellent material for such a way of praying; though one should not linger over obscure or difficult texts, but should be content with those verses which say something that one wants to say. Any formula of prayer in a book can be used in this way. One such book is *The Sufferings of Our Lord Jesus Christ*, by Fr. Thomas of Jesus, O.S.A. It is a translation of an old Portuguese work in which every second chapter is a prayer personally addressed to Our Lord. We hope to see this book reprinted shortly and distributed through the Mercier Press. Another way of dealing with this difficulty is to use a spiritual book line by line to supply one with ideas, and then to form one's own acts as a result of the few lines just read. Care must be taken, however, that this exercise does not develop into mere reading. The book used should be one which lends itself to such treatment, preferably an old friend, for if one has not read it before, the tendency will be to run on rapidly to see what comes next. Some books are written deliberately to carry one on; others have the knack of making one stop and think. Each man has to choose his own fare in this matter.

Aridity and distraction beset many men in prayer. They may have many different causes, but they always make the prayer burdensome, and soon the temptation arises to give up such "prayer" as sheer waste of time and to devote the period to "more useful" purposes.   This is the parting of the ways, and the beginning of the end of the spiritual life— if one yields permanently to that temptation.   One must react promptly by a vigorous *decision* never to give up the daily attempt at prayer, no matter how futile the whole thing may seem.   Without seeking further justification for such a decision—and it would not be hard to find many good reasons for it—one can throw full responsibility for the time thus employed on the Canon Law of the Church, (cf. Canon 125).   Because of that Canon we know that the daily attempt to pray is God's will.   Now we cannot improve upon God's plan or upon His way of doing things, and if we do things His way, He takes full responsibility for the results.   In any case, we cannot be His friends if we refuse to carry out His will, and His will is in the Code. For a priest the time of mental prayer is a daily appointment with God.   If God decides not to come, that is His business; our business is to keep the appointment and we shall not lose by faithfully doing so.

The causes of distraction and aridity at prayer are manifold. Distractions can arise from inordinate attachments, excessive pre-occupation with one's work, lack of sufficient remote preparation for prayer by spiritual reading, want of a generous effort at the beginning of our prayer to turn our *whole* attention to what we are going to do, and from many other such causes. If the cause is evident —well, one cures a disease by removing the cause. However, the nature of the human mind is such that distractions are almost inevitable; even the very interest of the subject of one's prayer may produce distractions according to the usual laws of the association of ideas. It is well, too, to remember that, as one progresses in prayer, a period comes wherein God changes His way of co-operation with the soul: He no longer acts on the intellect or the imagination, and thus these faculties run free and uncontrolled. Therefore, there are distractions that one cannot remove. What, then, is to be done? Either make the distraction a matter of prayer, or else just look over its shoulder as one does in a crowd when a stranger gets in one's line of sight. Leave the distractions there, but attend to God; the very difficulty of doing so makes the prayer more meritorious. Much of our dissatisfaction with our attempts at prayer arises from the fact that we are really trying to please ourselves instead of trying to please God.

This is also the reason why we are so discontented with arid prayer; it gives us no self-satisfaction. Aridity can arise in different ways. Over-indulgence in pleasure—even in lawful pleasure—worldliness, or sinful habits, can destroy our taste for the things of God. *The sensual man perceiveth not the things that are of the Spirit of God,* (1 Cor. ii, 14). Prayer is closely connected with the desire for God, with the relish and "taste" for God, and here again we see the close connection between the whole spiritual life and our prayer. However aridity does not always arise from infidelity, nor can it always be ascribed to fatigue, though the latter cause is, of course, sometimes operative. But, as we noted above, progress in prayer may lead to an arid state. To reach the Promised Land we must go out into the desert and leave the flesh-pots of Egypt, even though "flesh-pots" in this case have been spiritual. For a fuller treatment of this condition we would refer the reader to either of two books: *The Science of Prayer* by Fr. de Besse, O.F.M. Cap., or *On Prayer* by Fr. de Caussade, S.J. Here we can only warn the reader not to assume that such aridity is a sign of failure in prayer. It is often the reverse. In this case a man has reached the stage where he can only pray in complete dryness by patience and by faith, but whatever happens, the attempt at prayer must not be given up. Each and every priest must convince himself that he cannot relinquish this daily attempt at prayer without grave loss to himself and to the Church. Mental prayer has many important aspects. There is one, however, which is unique. Practically all the other exercises of the spiritual life can be performed by a priest who still clings to his own pet plans for doing his own will, whether it be a habit of deliberate venial sin, a refusal to listen to the promptings of grace, or a determination to refuse God something which God wants him to give up. A man can blind his own conscience to the serious danger of mortal sin—he may even go farther—and still carry out all his other religious exercises and duties. *But he cannot persist in any such infidelity and still persevere in the daily practice of mental prayer.* One thing or the other must give way. No man can look God in the face every day and say "No" to Him, and no man who has *not* a deliberate intention of saying "No" to God, need be afraid to look Him in the face. We may be weak and faint-hearted, but He is our Saviour; He knows the clay of which we are made, and the Scripture tells us *our sufficiency is from God.*

There is another point which should be made in this connection; we live in the world and to some extent we share its ways; we live in a particular nation and we share its national character and special outlook. To some extent we are all moulded by our environment. No matter how excellent all these influences may be, they have at least the defects of their merits. It is not for an Irish writer to analyze the American outlook and temperament. But perhaps this much may be said without giving offence: all we English-speaking peoples share a culture which has been moulded to a very great extent by Protestantism and which is now being greatly influenced by paganism. We priests have to stand between men and God; we have to lead men to God, and we *cannot* help men to escape from the prison of their own time and culture if we ourselves are in the same chains. To change the simile, we cannot guide men through the fog that besets the path of our ship if we ourselves have not some means of knowing the true course, either by experience, by wirelessed information, or by an occasional glimpse of the heavens.

If we do not daily make personal contact with our Lord, we shall easily become prisoners of our own time and our own surroundings. To a priest, the world should be at best "provincial"; for the priest's capital is elsewhere. If we do not sustain our supernatural outlook, we ourselves shall become as petty and as provincial as the parish-pump. Daily prayer and reflective reading are our only hope. Pius X devotes a great part of his *Letter to Catholic Priests*[1] to the question of daily prayer and reflection. His words must be quoted:

Let us hold it as a fundamental truth, that if a priest wishes to live up to the standard required by his position and his calling, he must give himself with intense earnestness to prayer. It is much to be deplored that prayer is too often made rather out of routine than with fervour of spirit, the psalms for the appointed Hours are recited listlessly, a few invocations are added, and no other time is set apart daily to commune with God with the piety which lifts the heart heavenward. . . .

It is of capital importance with regard to prayer that a certain time be set aside every day to meditate on things eternal. No priest can omit this without being guilty of great carelessness—and without grave loss to his soul. And in reference to the very danger we have just indicated, that of a priest becoming infected with spirit of his surroundings, the Pope writes:

*A certain heavenly-mindedness befits the priest, as being one who must himself know, speak of, and breathe unto others the love of heavenly things. . . . That daily meditation helps more than anything else to produce and sustain this habit of mind, this almost natural union with God, is so obvious to the thinking mind that we need insist no further upon it. A sad proof of this necessity is found in the lives of those priests who despise and make light of this practice. They are men in whom that priceless blessing—*sensus Christi*—has grown feeble; they give themselves wholly to vain and earthly things, fulfilling their sacred obligations negligently, coldly, and perhaps unworthily.*

Even in our ministry we shall reap the reward of our daily reading, our reflection, and our prayer. Therein lies the secret of that unction in preaching by which a man moves souls to come to God. Therein, too, is found the source of those happy inspirations that put just the right words into a priest's mouth when he is dealing with those in suffering or in sin. The words of Pope Pius X are to the point:

[1] 4.8.08; English translation, B.O.W. 1918.

Among those who fail to consider in the heart, or who look upon mental prayer as a burden there are some, who, though aware of the consequent spiritual atrophy, excuse themselves on the plea that it is manifestly to the advantage of others that they should be wholly taken up with the distractions and cares of the ministry. They make a sad mistake, for, not being accustomed to commune with God, when they speak to others of Him or try to instruct them in Christianity, the Divine Spirit breathes not through them, and the Gospel in their hands, seems almost without life. Their voice, however striking, prudent or eloquent it may be, is not the voice of the Good Shepherd, to which the sheep hearken to their salvation; it is but empty noise and passing vanity, often bearing fruit only in pernicious example, to the discredit of religion and the scandal of the good. So also is it with the whole life of such a man; it produces no solid fruit, at least only a short lived one, since there is lacking that heavenly shower which "the prayer of him that humbleth himself" calls down in great abundance. These are not the words of any retreat preacher, who might conceivably be led by zeal to overstate his case. They are the measured, solemn assertion of the Vicar of Christ addressing all his priests. Their authority alone should be sufficient to assure every priest of the value of his attempt at mental prayer, and to encourage him to spend time and trouble in its development. Those who have neglected prayer will find that they come to God as would a stranger to the managing director, carrying out the plans of one whom they have never met personally. Our Lord's desire is otherwise: *You are My Friends . . . !* Let not the reader be impatient with our insistence on prayer and friendship with God. We have quite a number of "dont's" to urge at a later stage, but since we dread negative spirituality, we do not want to empty a man's life of any of its pleasure without being ready to propose some better alternative. The personal friendship of Jesus can compensate for many sacrifices and that personal friendship can grow only by contact in prayer. Let us never forget His promise to the Apostles—that if they gave up certain joys of this world, they should have instead *a hundredfold in this life* and eternal life hereafter. Mental prayer is the gate to that **hundredfold.**

THE DIVINE OFFICE

ONE COULD WRITE almost indefinitely on Mental Prayer and Spiritual Reading, but there is another type of prayer which is of capital importance for the priest—the Divine Office. Here again, instead of trying to provide detailed solutions of the difficulties encountered which, to be effective, should be varied to meet the needs of each individual case— we intend rather to try to indicate an attitude in which to approach the Divine Office, and to be content with making a few suggestions as to details.

To our mind, the proper approach to the Divine Office, as to all the other points of the spiritual life, is closely connected with a right appreciation of the doctrine of the Mystical Body of Christ. We hope to deal with that subject later; here we must refer to the prayer of the Whole Christ. St. Augustine speaks of Christ as "one man who reaches to to the ends of the earth", (*In Ps.* 142); "There is but one man who reaches unto the end of time, and those that cry out are always His members", (*In Ps.* 85). The Mystical Christ, of Whom we are members, is conceived as extending throughout all space and all time. The "Whole Christ," to use St. Augustine's words,—Head and members—may be regarded as one Mystical Person, in the sense that while each member retains his own individuality and responsibility, there is a mutual sharing of merits and de-merits, of prayers and of sufferings throughout the whole Mystical Body. We can call the merits of Christ our own. He has taken upon Himself the shame and the punishment of our sins; and there is a sort of *communicatio idiomatum* between the Head and the members. The subject is too wide and too difficult to expound here, and we hope we shall be forgiven for referring the reader to what we have written elsewhere. But we must insist that all Christianity consists essentially in an "entering-in" to Christ, a "putting-on" of Christ, an identification with Christ,—an abiding in Christ as the branch abides in the vine. Now this union is not a mere static thing; it is something vital. Further, the Mystical Christ is four-dimensional in the sense that while in the human three-dimensional person the actions of any member can be referred to the whole person as he exists in a particular moment, the actions of Christ can be referred to, and "owned" by, a member at any time, however distant from the days of Christ.

Now the Divine Office is an entering into the prayer of Christ; it is a putting-on of the prayer of Christ; it is an identification with the prayer of Christ; it is an abiding in the Vine. Therefore, when the priest opens his breviary, he "enters into" the prayer of Christ in a much more real way than a monk, coming into choir where the office is being sung, "enters-in" to the prayer of the community. It is the prayer of Christ that the priest is praying. Christ is praying in him; he is praying in Christ. He is praying in the name of Christ and in the name of each of His members. In fact in a sense each of Christ's members is praying in the priest, and many of the sentiments expressed in the Psalms refer not to the priest but to Christ Himself and to some of His members, whose prayer they express.

The Office then is not a *personal* prayer; it is pre-eminently a *Christian* prayer and a *Catholic* prayer—it is the prayer of Christ. To quote St. Augustine: "We pray to Him in the form of God; He prays in the form of the slave, i.e. ourselves. There He is the Creator; here He is in the creature. He changes not, but takes the creature and transforms it into Himself, making us one man, Head and body, with Himself. We pray therefore to Him, and through Him, and in Him; we pray with Him, and in Him; we pray with Him and He with us; we recite this prayer of the Psalms in Him and He recites it in us", (*In Ps.* 85). And elsewhere St. Augustine writes: "Let Him rise up, this one chanter; let this man sing from the heart of each of us, and let each one of us be in this man. When each of you sings a verse, it is still this one man that sings, since you are all one in Christ. We do not say: 'To Thee, O Lord, we have lifted up our eyes,' but 'To Thee have I lifted up my eyes', (*Ps.* 122: 1). You should of course, consider that each of you is speaking but that primarily this one man is speaking Who reaches to the ends of the earth", (*In Ps.* 142). Here is the secret of the proper recitation of the Office. It is not so much a question of understanding the words that are to be said, as of appreciating the One Who is saying them. It is not so much a matter of stirring up one's own personal devotion, but rather of "putting-on" the devotion of Him in Whose name the prayer is said. In the unity of Christ, there is no distinction of "his" and "mine." All His is mine! And it is His prayer that I am to say from my breviary, for I am a branch of the Vine that is Christ. The importance of this way of viewing the Divine Office can hardly be exaggerated. Once it is properly understood and appreciated, there can be no more room for the usual criticism of the duty of saying the Office: that the text is too obscure to be understood, that the language is unfamiliar, that there is no help or scope for private devotion, that the office is out-of-date and out of harmony with the spirit and the needs of the times, etc., etc. Even if these objections were true—which we do not admit— they do not upset the paramount claim of the Divine Office to be *par excellence* the prayer of the priest. There is but one Priest—Christ Himself; we are but participators in His priesthood. So too, there is one great Prayer of that Priest; and, after the Mass, there is no other way in which we can make that Prayer so much our own, as in the Divine Office. It is true that the words of the Office do not always apply to our own personal dispositions or circumstances; they may even seem inapplicable to the mood of the moment. But they are intended to have a much wider application than that. They apply to some member of the Mystical Body of Christ in Whose name we are praying. We praise God on behalf of all creation; we thank Him, we beg His grace and mercy, not merely for ourselves, but for all mankind—in a word, for the Body of Christ. We must always remember, too, that the Psalms and Canticles which form such a large part of the Office, are the work of the Holy Spirit, Who is the Soul of the Mystical Body. The whole Office is drawn up by the Church, who is the Spouse of Christ and who in this has the special aid of Her Divine Head. So that this prayer itself—apart from the One Who prays—has an intrinsic value that makes it more pleasing to God than any other prayer which human ingenuity or devotion might contrive. When we further remember that the priest says the Office as the official representative of the Church, we see the force of the blunt remark that, "When a priest opens his breviary—no matter what sort of man he may be—the Almighty has just got to listen!" The apparent lack of reverence in this remark disappears when we recollect that it is merely a forcible way of stressing the supernatural character of the Office and the "ambassadorial" character of the one who recites it.

There is no other vocal prayer in which the "priestly" function is so well exercised. A priest may be said to be one who speaks to men in the name of God, and to God in the name of men. In the pulpit and the confessional he does the former; the latter function he exercises especially in the Divine Office. Nor must it be thought that this representative prayer is a mere formality, a relic of medievalism, something which has lost its real significance and is no longer of practical importance. Let us reiterate clearly and forcibly: after the sacrifice of the Mass, there is nothing a priest can do for the souls in his charge so effectively as to recite the Divine Office in their name. There is no prayer which comes so near to acting *ex opere operato*, and in which so little is left of the *operans*. It is a putting-on of the prayer of Christ Himself, and our failure to appreciate it is really a result of our failure to have the "mind of Christ" in us. In this connection, we must never forget the principle noted in our first chapter with regard to the priest's part in the mediation of grace. Despite the infinite merits of Christ's prayers and sufferings, despite the incalculable influence of Our Lady, there still remains something to be "filled-up" in prayer and suffering on behalf of the Church by its members. The Divine Office is *par excellence* the way for each priest to fill up the Prayer of Christ for His Body the Church, and in particular for the priest's own flock. Of such practical importance is this function, that we would be tempted to think that, if there be anything wrong in the parish, the first enquiry to make as to its cause, would be to ask how does the Pastor say his Mass and Office! That perhaps is an exaggeration, but it contains a truth that is often forgotten. A more practical and detailed discussion of how to say the Office needs a further chapter. Let us finish this one by a rather daring and somewhat exaggerated comparison—for the orthodox interpretation of which we rely on the theological acumen of our readers. We might compare the private prayer of the priest to the offering of the bread and wine before the consecration, and the recital of the Divine Office to the offering of the consecrated species afterwards. It is true that the difference is not so clear-cut or so complete, but there is something of "Christ" in the Divine Office that no amount of private "devotion" can achieve. Our Lord's last message to His priests must never be forgotten; if we are to bring forth fruit, it must be by abiding in Him. There are few more certain ways of abiding in Him than by saying the Office. If we approach it in that attitude, a lot of its difficulty will vanish.

THE OFFICE—THE PRAYER OF CHRIST

EVERY PRIEST HAS HEARD of—and tried—many devices that might help him to say the Office well; to have an intention for each hour, or even each psalm, to associate each hour with some mystery of Our Lord's life and death; to visualize the Saint of the day, or the Angels or Our Lady or even Our Lord Himself as saying the Office with him. Such plans may be used in so far as they prove to be helpful; for many, however, they soon fail to help, and ultimately may even become a hindrance. First of all one must allow oneself sufficient time to say the Office properly. While many priests find that a brisk recitation is necessary to avoid distractions, precipitancy is always an enemy of devotion. The place, too, is a difficult matter. The ideal of course would be to recite it before the Blessed Sacrament, but this is not always practical, and so the sound rule is to say the Office in the way one finds best. There are some who can be quite recollected in the middle of a crowd; others must have peace and quiet. Some men find that an effort to preserve external "recollection" is a distraction from internal recollection while others know that their only hope is to preserve a proper exterior attitude. This problem, like those of duration and of fixing a set time each day for the Office, is difficult, but they all must be faced and settled with decision. We grant the innumerable difficulties, but where there is a will there is a way. We shall discuss the finding of the will further down, and, that found, we are confident that the way will find itself. It is of course impossible, even if there were time enough, to follow in detail all the thoughts of all the psalms. One could, however, decide to say one hour, or one nocturn each day, a little more slowly than the rest; the particular part being varied from week to week. Alternatively, one could pause at a particular verse in each psalm—an 'old friend' with an old friend's message and association, and these pet verses could be marked as they come to one's notice. It is excellent to associate each psalm with one or two particular verses and to let the idea of those verses occupy one's mind for the whole psalm. The question of attention may be dealt with

in that way. There is, of course, no need to remind readers
of the doctrine of St. Thomas on attention: we may attend to
the saying of the Office, to the things said, or to the Person
to Whom they are said. In regard to the Office we may add
a fourth possibility—that of attending to the Person Who is
really saying the Office.

This, to our mind, is the cardinal point of the whole
question, and it is due to the fact that we overlook it that
most of our problems arise. If our habitual attitude with
regard to the Office is correct, and if we start the Office
properly, the rest should look after itself. Of our attitude,
we have already said something; now let us consider how to
start the Office. The Office itself gives us the answer to this
question. It opens with an appeal to God to hasten to our
aid, and then immediately asserts the purpose of our
prayer and petition, by the Gloria Patri. Thus the Divine
Office should commence with a spiritual communion, which
can hardly be better formulated than in its own opening
words: *Deus, in adjutorium meum intende; Domine, ad adjuvandum
me festina.* The sincerity of this petition is what matters.
It implies a realization of the inadequacy of our own prayer
and a true zeal for the glory of God: it rises from a lively
sense of our need for union with Christ Who alone can give
adequate praise and glory to the Blessed Trinity, from a
loyal sharing of His "mind," and a confident trust in His
merits and pleasingness in the sight of the Father. How
completely the sentiments are part of the priest depends
greatly upon his spiritual life.

We have already indicated some of the methods of
developing this interior life. Let us here summarize the
result of some future discussions, by saying that the fundamental virtues required for the Divine Office are those
required for every other part of the spiritual life, namely,
faith, hope, charity, humility, and abandonment to the will
of God. We must have faith; without it, we do not know
God, we do not see any value in prayer, we are ignorant
of our share of Christ's merits, we cannot realize that all
the work of our ministry is a supernatural one dependent
on grace and upon those means by which grace is brought
down to earth. We must have hope; without it prayer is
but folly. We must have charity, for without charity all

else profiteth nothing. It is only the love of God that can properly animate us in His service; and it is especially necessary for the Divine Office, for there is less room there for the gratification of self-love by our own activity and success than there is in some of the more active works. This charity must manifest itself in the love of our neighbours. Otherwise we lie. So true is this of the Divine Office, that we must commence its recitation not only by a communion with Christ, our Head and Saviour, but also by a communion with our neighbour—with the members of Christ, with those whom He wishes to save. Unless we say the Office in union with Christ and in His Name, it is fruitless. Unless we say the Office in union with the members of Christ, much of it is often meaningless. That is why so much of the Office seems affected and futile; we are saying it in our own name and for ourselves, instead of in the name of, and for the whole Christ.

When we open the Breviary, we must try to realize that we are entering in to a choir, in to a congregation, in to a society, in to a unity made up of souls of every condition on earth together with souls in heaven and souls in purgatory. The Office will never have anything like its true meaning for us until we say it in this way—that is, until we say it as priests, not as private individuals. The opening of the Breviary should be a "transfiguration" of the priest. At that moment we should put on the merits and power of Christ, and the needs and weaknesses of our fellow-men. To regard the office merely as a tedious obligation which must be discharged, or to expect that its primary effect and purpose should be our own spiritual development and "edification" is quite wrong and unpriestly. The Office is said for the edification of Christ, for His "building-up" and formation in the souls of all men; and above all for the glory of God. We should turn to the Office as to a most potent means of supplying for our own cheerfully recognized inadequacy to pray on behalf of our neighbour or to give glory to God. Only then will we be content with the text of the Breviary, for even though it seems without "point" for us, it gives expression to the needs of our neighbour and is full of value for God. It is, in fact, the voice of His well-beloved Son in Whom He is well-pleased.

With these sentiments, we may find it easier to devote sufficient time to the Office to say it properly. There is no need to summarize the enormous calls made upon every moment in the day of a priest, or to stress the need for leaving him as much time as possible to devote to his ministry. We grant all that. But it is precisely because a priest's time is so valuable and because his responsibilities are so weighty that he must be generous in devoting time to his Breviary. God is God. He demands the first fruits and the best of the flock. To offer Him in sacrifice only what is "left-over" is almost an insult. The truth is that if the fundamental motive of our life is zeal for God's glory, we shall be generous in giving time to His direct praise in the Office; we shall desire to give Him as large a share as possible in our work in His vineyard; we shall be earnest in calling down His grace in all our efforts; and we shall prefer that the fruits of our work should come through prayer rather than through our own personal skill and activity. Whereas if it be zeal for our own glory that animates us in the service of God, then we shall rather despise the Breviary, wish to devote all our time to active works, and resent all that lessens our personal sense of achievement. Every priest should take as his slogan the words of St. John the Baptist: "He must increase—I must decrease." If our zeal be true, we shall readily admit that without Him we can do nothing; we shall gladly glory in our infirmities that the power of Christ may dwell in us; and we shall realize that precisely because there is so much to be done and so little time in which to do it, we must devote all the time we can to imploring His co-operation in our ministry.

Perhaps the root of the whole matter is that we forget our fundamental principles. God created the world for His glory, and our primary duty as creatures, but more especially as Christians and priests, is to give Him that glory which is His due. We priests are sometimes impatient at having to recite long verses of praise and worship when there is so much work to be done for souls. We forget that in thus praising God we are discharging in a most efficient manner, one of the primary purposes of our creation and of our priesthood. This sacrifice of praise is at all times due to

God, but it has a special urgency in an age when the forces of "anti-God" are openly organized and publicly reviling His Name. A sounder sense or perspective would enable us to take a more correct view of the relative importance of such direct service of God by praise and worship and the less direct service by the cure of souls. Both are our duty; but neither one dispenses us from the other. Above all let us never forget that in the Christian restoration we are to sing a new Canticle. The new Canticle is Christ—through Whom and with Whom and in Whom is all the glory of God. In the Divine Office we put on Christ, Who as the Divine Word is the eternal Canticle that God sings in the ecstasy of His Own Goodness. Is it any wonder that St. Benedict calls the Divine Office the "*Opus Dei*"? In it we share in the work that is God's own life and beatitude.

SINCERITY IN OUR SACRIFICE

THE CENTRAL ACT of the life of the priest, in which all else reaches its culmination and from which all else should flow, is the Sacrifice of the Mass. Let us prescind for the moment from the extraordinary nature of the Victim offered in the Mass and of the Priesthood in which we share, and merely consider the act of offering sacrifice to God. St. Augustine says: "Every visible sacrifice is a sign of invisible sacrifice," and St. Thomas insists: "The sacrifice which is offered externally, represents the inward spiritual sacrifice by which the soul offers itself to God.". . . . The outward sacrifice is the manifestation of the inward sacrifice by which "a man offers himself to God, as the First Cause of his being, as the principle of his activity and the object of his beatitude," (*cf. Cont. Gen. iii.* 120).

A sacrifice, in fact, says something by an action. The "something" is predetermined; it arises from the nature of God and the relations which His creatures should have towards Him. When we offer a sacrifice we must mean what we say; otherwise our enacted statement is a lie and a mockery. What then does a priest say by sacrifice to God ? He says in effect that God is God, and that he, the priest, gladly recognizes God's sovereignty, God's goodness, God's rights. He asserts that he is completely subject to God— that he, and every moment of his day, are completely at God's disposal.

A whole plan of the spiritual life could be derived from this statement as a starting point. The sincerity of that repeated sacrificial assertion depends upon the degree to which our actions and dispositions during the day are in accordance with the promises and the assertions which we make in the morning by offering sacrifice to God. Now we all know that we are human and liable to fall seven times a day. We renounce sin every time we go to confession, and yet we fall again before the end of the week, so that if there be some discrepancy between our promise and our perform-ance, we cannot immediately assert that our promise was insincere. But, just as in the case of the penitent there is a sharp distinction between the failure to keep a sincere promise through human frailty, and the failure to keep a promise which was insincere from the very start, so too there are differences in our failures to fulfil our sacrificial promise.

It is with this distinction in mind—a distinction familiar to every priest who hears confessions—that we should examine our day to see how it agrees with the promise made by our sacrifice. Let us be quite clear about it. For the moment we are leaving aside the part played by Christ as the Priest and as the Victim in the Mass; we are leaving aside the fact that all worship and service is to be given to God through Christ. We are simply concentrating our attention on the fact that, as priests, we are men who daily offer sacrifice to God in so far as in us lies. If that sacrifice means anything, surely it means that we are living by God and for God, and not by ourselves or for ourselves; it means that we are giving ourselves completely to God—not only at the time of our ritual offering, but throughout the whole day. This is an important point for every priest, for it means that each of us daily makes a ritual promise to God of self-immolation, and this promise is not fulfilled merely by giving other souls to Him. We must give Him our own *self*. No matter how fruitful our day may be—or may seem to be—in good works, in conversions, in apostolic triumphs, yet our daily sacrifice— considered merely as a personal sacrifice for the moment, and prescinding from the intrinsic value and dignity of the August Victim offered in the Mass—our daily sacrifice is a mockery, if we do not also, and before all else, give ourselves to God *even in our work*.

This is an important point. There can be very many different motives animating our work for souls. It is possible to approach the work of the ministry in almost the same spirit as the non-Catholic regards his career or his business. We want to make the grade, we want to be a "success," we want to show others what we can do, we want the applause either of ourself or our fellowmen. We feel justified if we "deliver the goods."

But let us here observe that Christ delivered *Himself;* and although His thirst for souls is beyond all telling, yet it is safe to say that it takes second place to His zeal for His Father's glory. His first act on becoming man was to offer Himself to God—by accepting God's will in its entirety—as a substitute for the sacrifices and holocausts which were so deficient in God's eyes. And that disposition animated all His actions.

Such must be our attitude and disposition also—quite apart from any connection with our work or with the souls committed to our care. As priests, we must never forget the First Commandment. As priests, we must never forget that we are men who have publicly offered sacrifice to God and that we have said to God formally and ritually that He is God and we are His creatures that we are at His disposal and that His will is the law of our life. Obviously we must mean what we say. It is true that the obligations which this act imposes on us will arise with fresh force when we come to consider our relations with Christ both as priests and as Christians. But even as creatures who offer sacrifice, we owe God the carrying out of what we have promised. How are we to fulfil this promise? How are we to make good this ritual statement of complete dependence and donation? First of all, by Faith, Hope and Charity. These virtues need separate treatment and we shall consider them later. After these, almost all else can be summed up in Humility and Obedience to God's will.

In the course of this work, we shall frequently come back to humility as—in practice—the fundamental virtue of the spiritual life, even though charity is the essence of it. We shall also consider both humility and abandonment in their own place. But we want to stress here the connection between true humility and our sacerdotal sacrifice. Quite apart from our dependence on Christ for our priestly powers, and from our dependence upon Him as Victim to supply for the shortcomings of our own personal sacrifice, we are still obliged as priests to be specially humble. For all we have is from God. Our existence, our life, our faculties, our ability, our health—our all—come from Him. They are *on loan*—so to speak—even though it be a permanent loan, but they belong to God. We assert our debt and dependence, and acknowledge it, by offering sacrifice to Him. Every action even, depends upon Him for its initiation and its performance; we cannot perform a single act without His co-operation. Again we acknowledge that by our daily sacrifice. How then could we behave as if all were our own—

as if we were the source of all the good that we have or do ?
How then could we glory in our own success ?

Not only have we acknowledged by offering sacrifice that
all this comes from God, but we have also given ourselves
to God. A very practical test, then, of the sincerity of our
sacrifice and of the harmony between it and our daily
actions can be found when circumstances, or even the
arrangements of ecclesiastical superiors, hinder—or seem
to hinder—the work of our ministry. Then, if we really
mean what we say to God by offering sacrifice—that we
are completely at His disposal—we shall accept this
"pruning," this frustration, in the same way as our Divine
Model accepted all His Father's "arrangements." If, on
the contrary, we are really seeking self in the service of God,
then we shall be liable to murmuring, rebellion, anger and
impatience, and all the other displays of wounded self-love.
Granted that our duty to God has a special reference to zeal
for souls; yet that zeal must take second place to our zeal
for God's glory. This latter zeal should show itself in
humility and abandonment to God's will. In fact, if one
should try to sum up in one word the correct attitude of a
man who has offered sacrifice to God, that one word would
be *patience*. For, if we are priests, we are also in a sense,
victims, and patience is the true manifestation of our
devotion to God. May we here refer again to the pregnant
phrase we quoted from Pius X in the first chapter as a
slogan for the priest: "*Idem velle, idem nolle*"? This patient
acceptance of God's will in all its manifestations is one of
the best acts of true reverence to God, our Sovereign Lord.
But to patience, we must add confidence. We offer sacrifice
to testify that God is God; we therefore assert our conviction
of His infinite Goodness. It is true that our confidence will
find a new support when we consider the dignity of the
Divine Victim we offer in the Mass, but even apart from that,
we should be prepared to abandon ourselves to the infinite
Goodness of God in all the manifestations of His will, just
as Our Master said on the Cross: "*Into Thy hands, O Lord, I
commend My Spirit.*" By doing so we give further testimony
to our belief in His Goodness.

Too much stress cannot be laid upon the necessity of
zeal for God's glory as a predominant note in the outlook

of every priest. A priest should be as careful of God's glory as he is in handling any holy thing which belongs to God. He should be almost as quick to repress all attempts to steal God's glory as he would be to repress all irreverence to the Blessed Sacrament. This is an overstatement, but it only emphasizes a truth. This same zeal should lead him to shun all deliberate self-glorification and counting of his own "gains." It is the tendency to write our own names upon the good works we do in God's service, by His grace, that hinders so much the success of our ministry. When we have succeeded anywhere we tend to call ourselves fine fellows, but Our Lord told us to say we are unprofitable servants even if we should succeed everywhere. The importance of humility, and its urgent necessity for our life as priests, is so great that it demands special treatment in a later chapter. It has a close connection with our zeal for God's glory, which, with an appreciation of God's infinity, will make us dissatisfied with any personal sacrifice that we can make to God. The utter inadequacy of our own sacrifice, and of both our power and our performance in His service, will make us look for something more worthy of Him, something which will praise Him adequately and give us power to serve Him faithfully. This we will find in the Blessed Eucharist, and we shall consider that august Sacrament in our next chapter.

But we have deliberately chosen to approach it in this "Old Testament" fashion, looking forward, as it were, to the Redeemer Who is to come. It is an excellent way to approach our daily Mass: first to offer ourselves in sacrifice with the bread and wine, and then to seek for something more worthy of God in the Eucharistic Sacrifice. The riches of that Sacrifice are so great that we have first stressed the importance of our personal sacrifice, lest it should be overlooked and completely overshadowed in the Sacrifice Christ has left to us in the Mass. The infinite dignity of the New Priest and the New Victim Who there comes to our aid, should not let us be unmindful of the need for personal devotion and personal sacrifice to God on our own part. It is just possible for a priest to approach to an erroneous Luther-like attitude in this matter, feeling that it does not matter what his own dispositions are—it is the Mass that

matters. That in one sense is quite true. No personal
unworthiness in the priest can take away from the intrinsic
value of the Mass, but it can take away tremendously from
what the Mass applies to the priest. It can take away tremendously from the personal union of the priest with the
High Priest and Victim as Whose minister he acts. We must,
therefore, conform ourselves to the mind of Christ our Model,
and even though true zeal for God's glory will lead us to
seek divine aid in glorifying Him, yet it will not make us
unmindful of the need of our own personal devotion. By
any sacrifice we offer to God—if it be sincerely offered—we
assure Him of our complete acceptance of His Sovereignty
and our total submission to His Will; we commit ourselves to
a life of faith, hope, charity, humility and abandonment to
the will of our Father in Heaven.

THE MASS—THE SACRIFICE OF CHRIST

IN THE LAST CHAPTER, we considered the priest as a man who daily offers sacrifice to God, testifying his adoration, his complete dependence and his willing submission in God's regard. We abstracted completely from the Person of the High Priest in whose priesthood all others are but participators, and from the extraordinary nature of the sacrifice offered in the Mass on behalf of the whole Church. We merely stressed the fact that a priest offers sacrifice, and that to his exterior sacrifice there should correspond an interior sacrifice, which in turn demands that his whole life should tend to be in accord with the meaning of his sacrificial statement. For a sacrifice says something to God, and the priest offering sacrifice must mean what he says by it—not only at the moment of offering, but as a permanent and ruling disposition in his life.

We indicated how much this could mean for the whole life of a priest, but we reserved a fuller discussion until we had considered the tremendous additional force that our conclusions would acquire from the special nature of the sacrifice offered by the Catholic priest of the New Law in the sacrifice of the Mass. The Mass, according to St. Thomas and St. Augustine, is "the perfect sacrament of our Lord's Passion." That is to say, it is related to the Sacrifice of Calvary in somewhat the same way as the consecrated species are related to the Body and Blood of Christ. Just as the Blessed Sacrament gives the Body of Christ a new "location" in space and time, where It is really, truly and substantially—but "sacramentally"—present, so the double consecration at Mass gives the Sacrifice of Calvary a new location in space and time, where It also is really, truly and substantially—but "sacramentally"—present. In each case the Real Presence is effected and located by a "sign"—by the accidents of something else. The "accidents" of the consecration "locate" the sacrifice of the Cross. The Mass is Calvary in sacramental form, and the sacrifice we priests offer to God each morning is the sacrifice which Christ offered on Calvary. In our Lord's sacrifice on Calvary, we can distinguish an interior and an exterior sacrifice. The interior sacrifice of Himself was but the culminating act of a lifelong series of acts of complete devotion to God. In fact we are tempted to imagine Our Lord as summing up His whole life and love in one great act, and giving it exterior expression in the sacrifice of the Cross. His whole sacrifice, interior and exterior, He enshrined in the Sacrament of the Eucharist for our benefit. The Mass, therefore, contains all the spiritual realities of the Cross. St. Thomas puts it this way: "We do not say that Christ is daily crucified and killed (i.e. in the Mass), because both the acts of the Jews and the punishment of Christ are transitory. Yet those things which carry with them Christ's relation to God the Father are said to be done daily (in the Mass); these are, to offer, to sacrifice, and the like. On that account the victim is perpetual and was offered once by Christ in this manner that it might be daily offered by His members," (4 *Sent. XII*). We may safely assume that "those things which carry with them Christ's relation to God the Father" include supreme worship and love, perfect obedience and superabundant satisfaction for sin, in fact, the whole interior and exterior sacrifice of Christ. That is what we offer to God in the Mass. No wonder Trent tells us: "*The faithful of Christ can do no work more holy, more divine than this tremendous mystery,*" (*Sess.* xxii, c.2). It is then the most important act of the priest's life and we need not apologize for dwelling upon it. But let us first consider it in its relation to the priest's own interior life.

When a priest offers up the Mass, he offers it, of course, as a minister of Christ Who is the principal offerer, and is a representative of the whole Church—the Body of Christ. But that must not blind us to the fact that the priest offers up the sacrifice of the Mass as his own sacrifice also. He must, then, mean what the Mass says. Now the Mass is Our Lord's sacrifice, and expresses Our Lord's interior sacrifice which was, as we have shown, the summing-up and culmination of His whole life. So that in making the Mass his own, the priest has to make Our Lord's interior disposition his own too, and *he has to make those dispositions permeate his whole life.* The priest's position is somewhat the reverse of that of Our Lord. Our Lord first lived His life of perfect concordance with the will of God, and then summed it up in an interior

sacrifice which found expression in the exterior sacrifice of the
Cross. The priest "takes over" this sacrifice in the Mass
and makes it his own. He therefore has to endeavour to
make his interior sacrifice correspond with the exterior
sacrifice sacramentally renewed in the Mass, and he then
has to make his whole life correspond to that interior
sacrifice! If the figure of speech is not too irreverent, one
could say that our Lord's whole life and dispositions are
"telescoped" into His sacrifice on Calvary, which becomes
the sacrifice of the priest at Mass. The priest then has to
expand and apply that sacrifice to his whole life and
dispositions. It is true that, in the order of time, the Passion
of Christ is first applied to the soul of the priest at
Baptism—but even so, Baptism only looks forward to the
Blessed Eucharist; and—are we not baptized into the death
of Christ?! Each Mass, as it were, re-enacts and renews the
whole process.

Such a commitment—to live as Christ lived—would be
a terrifying obligation for any mere human being, but the
very sacrifice which lays so great an obligation on the priest
also gives him in the Communion, the strength and the
means to carry it out. "*I can do all things in Him who strengthen-
eth me,*" *(Phil. iv, 13).* "*I live, now no longer I, but Christ
it is who liveth in me,*" *(Gal. ii, 20).* There can, therefore, be no question of regarding a priest as a person
who merely brings the faithful to God by his preaching
and ministerial work, and for whom a life of devotion
is something to be desired but not essential, something to be recommended but not commanded. The very
sacrifice the priest offers—and this is his principal duty—
devotes him as completely to God as Our Lord Himself. If
a priest only knew it, his daily Mass is—as far as he is
concerned—more or less a deliberate lie if he be not
endeavouring to live a life of holiness. Of course, we all
know that the value of the Mass for the Church is quite
independent of the dispositions of the minister. But we also
know that the value of the Mass as applied to the priest
can be very dependent upon his own dispositions. It is
obvious then that as a personal sacrifice it could even be
meaningless if his own life and interior sacrifice do not in
some way correspond to what the Mass says. To develop

and emphasize this point we devoted the foregoing chapter to a consideration of the priest as a person who offers sacrifice. We wish to stress the fact that first, by offering any sacrifice to God he professes his complete devotion and submission to Him, and that secondly, by offering the sacrifice of the Mass he professes his willingness to be conformed to Christ in His sonship and service to the Father. St. Thomas sums up the point in discussing whether the priest should consume the sacrament at Mass. "Whoever offers a sacrifice should be a partaker (*particeps*) of the sacrifice, because the sacrifice which is offered externally is a sign of the interior sacrifice by which one offers oneself to God. Whence by the fact that he receives of the sacrifice he shows that he interiorly shares in the sacrifice," (Summa 3. 82. 4). And Pope Pius XI, in his Encyclical *Miserentissimus Deus,* insists that even the faithful should add their own acts to those of Our Lord: "*We must join together, in the august sacrifice of the Blessed Eucharist, the act of immolation made by the priest with that of the Faithful so that they too, may offer themselves up as 'a living sacrifice, holy and pleasing to God',* (*Rom. xii,* 1). *Therefore, St. Cyprian dared to affirm that 'the sacrifice of the Lord is not complete as far as our sanctification is concerned unless our offerings correspond to His Passion,'* " (Ep. 63, n. 381).

We once more stress the point that there is no question of making the intrinsic value of the Mass depend upon the personal dispositions of the priest. Our whole concern in this discussion is to determine what should be the life and dispositions of the priest in view of the fact that he offers the sacrifice of the Mass. The Mass renews the sacrifice of Calvary and makes it ours, this sacrifice is the perfect expression of our Lord's life and dispositions. If then the Mass is to be truly our sacrifice, we must so live that it is also a true expression of our life. To do this, we should offer ourselves at each Mass with the bread and wine at the offertory, accept in advance all that God's will disposes or permits for us during the day, and then endeavour to spend the rest of the day in accordance with those dispositions. This devotion to God's will has a wonderful reward, which is foreshadowed in the very sequence of events at Mass. Just as God changes the bread and wine offered up at Mass into the Body and Blood of Christ, so, too, He will, by His paternal providence and the sequence of events, effect our "consecration," our incorporation, our transformation into Christ. By doing the will of God, we shall abide in the Vine and become more and more closely united to our Head and High Priest. In pledge of that transformation, and in order to give us the strength to do and to suffer according to God's will, our Lord gives us His own Body and Blood as the Food of our souls in the communion of the Mass. In fact, if we may sum it up—when the priest offers himself up as a willing victim at the offertory, our Lord "says Mass" with him; that is, He accepts him as He accepts the bread and wine, and changes him by the gradual effect of His will into Himself. There is a deep significance in those words addressed to us priests at our ordination: *"Agnoscite quod agitis, imitamini quod tractatis!"* If we imitate our Lord in His devotion to the will of the Father, that will becomes for us an all-consuming fire—a transforming consecration which will make us one with Christ. Are not the very words of consecration: *"This is My Body"* ?

In His Encyclical on Reparation, Pius XI sums up the matter thus: *"In the degree to which our oblation and sacrifice will the more perfectly correspond to the sacrifice of our Lord, that is to say, to the extent that we have immolated love of self and our passions and crucified our flesh in that mystical crucifixion of which the Apostle writes, so much the more plentiful fruits of propitation and of expiation will we gain for ourselves and others."*

The Holy Father is writing for all the faithful, but his words apply with added force to us priests. Even as Christians we are baptized into the death of Christ, our "old man" has been sentenced to death and Christ has been born in our soul. Our life's work, even as Christians, is to carry out this death-sentence on ourself, so that Christ may live in us, in all our actions and in every moment of our lives. Every Mass we say or hear should remind us of this "conversion" from ourself to Christ. What we wrote of the Divine Office— as an "entering-in" to the prayer of Christ is only typical of the whole life of the Christian, but it is especially typical of the whole life of the priest, which must be an "entering-in" to the whole life of Christ. For Christ is our Way, our Truth, and our Life: He is our All. A fuller discussion of the significance of the Mass will be found in the present writer's book *This Tremendous Lover* from which we quote the following summary:

"Christ lived a life of complete and humble abandonment to the will of His Father. His whole life was one long interior sacrifice of himself to God. He gave ritual expression to this interior sacrifice by the external sacrifice of the Cross. He has given us this external sacrifice by the Mass and in the Mass, to express our interior sacrifice to God. This interior sacrifice of ours must then be like His—a sincere, humble and complete abandonment to the will of Our Father in Heaven, not only at the moment of the Mass, but in every moment of our lives."

VICTIMS WITH CHRIST

AS CHRISTIANS, we are men who have been baptized into the sacrificial death of Christ; as priests, we are men who daily offer that same sacrifice of Christ in sacramental form. In the Mass, as the present Holy Father tells us, Christ *"offers not only Himself as Head of the Church to the Heavenly Father, but in Himself His mystical members as well,"* (Encycl. on The Mystical Body). Each priest at Mass, as we urged in the previous chapter should add his personal offering of himself to that made by Christ—for by offering sacrifice, he protests publicly that he stands completely at God's disposal. If, then, we are sincere Christians and sincere priests, we shall imitate what we perform, we shall be partners and partakers not only with Christ as Priest, but also with Christ as Victim. In other words, we shall daily make our own the sentiments expressed by Our Lord on entering into the world—*"Behold I come that I may do Thy Will, O God!"* This involves a deliberate daily decision to accept the "body" God has fitted to us; to be what God wills us to be, to be a Christian, to be a priest, to be this particular priest, in this particular parish, with all these particular qualities, this history, these surroundings, obligations, successes and failures—with all, in fact, that God's Providence has arranged for us.

It may seem superfluous to stress this idea, yet it is often the starting-point of our failure to be all that a priest should be. There are many different roads that lead to the priesthood; there are many different points of view, many different tastes or hopes, and many different temperaments, that bring us to the work of the ministry; yet, once there, we have to take the priesthood as it is, not as we would like it, or as we thought it to be. To illustrate what is meant, let us take the case of the man who becomes a priest to save souls and envisages the priesthood as a life of direct—and successful—apostolic activity in various forms. He gets into a parish where everything seems to hamper his efforts; finance is bad, co-operation non-existent, prejudice rampant, and he falls foul of his own flock through mistaken zeal. Diocesan regulations tie his hands; even the

Bishop seems to stand between him and the success of his ministry. If his whole spiritual life is tied up with the successful saving of souls, his apparent failure to achieve this may mean the end of his fervour and the beginning of "trouble." On the contrary, if he accepts the priesthood as it really is—a participation in the priesthood of Christ with the *de congruo* obligation of self-sacrifice with Christ—he can and should integrate all his experience into his spiritual life. His efforts for souls are to be made as part of his work—as fulfilment of the offering he makes of himself at Mass. The fruit of his efforts depends on God. If God permits that there be no fruit—or at least no apparent fruit—well, that is God's business; while the priest's business is to do God's will. If regulations and circumstances hamper his activities—well, the nails hampered our Lord's activities on the Cross. Yet it is on the Cross that Christ saves the whole of mankind. That is the essence of His redeeming work; the rest is only an integral part; and if Christ deigns to share the essential part of His priesthood with us, can we complain?

To a man living an interior life, all things can work together for good; and no failure in the ministry is for him really a failure. Apart from sin, his worst failures will be his greatest success, for it is by abiding in Christ that His apostles are to bring forth fruit, and there is no better way of abiding in Christ than by doing the will of God. A somewhat similar difficulty appears when a priest is faced with making efforts on behalf of souls, out of all proportion to the extent of the possible harvest, or to the probability of reaping it. If he is a man who measures the value of his work by its immediate and apparent fruits, he will quickly lose heart, he will give up trying, and he may soon cease to be generous with God. But if he lives in accordance with his morning sacrifice, he will spend himself in his ministry as far as prudence will allow, especially when he recalls that all he does for a single soul is done for Christ, even though his efforts lead nowhere. There is no need to examine all the various possibilities. Each priest can work out the idea for himself, and most of us know what frustration means. If, however, a man will but regard his day's work and experiences as the implementation of his sacrificial offering of himself together with Christ at Mass, nothing can separate him from the love of God. In this St. Paul is both a model and a master, who but repeats the practice and the preaching of the Divine Master.

Yet another point: This daily decision "to be a priest" has an importance in another way. It is true that as ordination approached, most of us more less definitely cut ourselves off from all that we felt was foreign to the priesthood. But as time went on, we found that our notions of the obligations of a priest could be modified in the light of our own and others' experience. If, then, at the time of ordination, we had accepted some of the obligations with reluctance, this reserve tends to show itself later on in a lowering of our standards and a compromise with our desires. Now it cannot be denied that every prudent man has to learn by experience and has to adjust his notions accordingly. Views that are too strict have to be eased a little, lest the too tightly stretched strings should snap; defences that are found weak must be strengthened. But under guise of this prudent adjustment there can creep in a compromise with the world—with the "old man"—that may lead to very regrettable consequences. That is where the daily renewal of our sacrifice can operate to check rapine in the holocaust. Every priest needs recreation and relaxation. His amusement and his pleasures are limited to some extent by diocesan law and custom, as well as by the danger of scandal and of excess. Now there should be no tampering with these limits. Even if they do not seem to be necessary in our own particular case, yet they should be observed as part of our sacrificial promise, as a means of being united with Christ. *"He that abideth in Me. . . . !"*

There is another aspect of our self-sacrifice which needs frequent examination and renewal. Having given ourselves completely to God, we should be ever on our guard against vain glory, empty ambition, avarice, the desire for notoriety, or popularity; in particular, against envy and jealousy of our colleagues' success, which should never be allowed to take possession of us. We have laid ourselves down on the altar with and in Christ, and if God chooses to strip us of those things that many men prize, He is not only taking us at our word, He is also fitting us for a heavenly crown of unspeakable glory, and conforming us to the image of His Son. This is a point that must never be forgotten. Just as the Communion is the final action in the sacrifice that commenced with the Offertory, so is union with Christ the final result of our offering of ourself to God in practice as well as in word during the day. It is by doing the will of God that we truly live up to our title of "Father", and indeed our Lord told us that by doing the will of God we become His mother. The whole of His address at the Last Supper is a tender plea for union with Him in every moment of our lives.

It is not easy to avoid being vague here. We are trying to urge a new attitude to the old routine; to widen the notion of a priest's vocation so as to include self-sacrifice and a share in Christ's Victimhood as its principal part, rather than the more limited view which confines it to an active and successful ministry in the service of souls. If this wide view is once adopted everything else falls into its place and is found reasonable and useful. But it is not easy to bring oneself to adopt this view. It means renouncing all self-centred activity; it means an equal readiness to do little things for God as to do great things for Him. The test of the sincerity of our devotion to God is found in our willingness to serve Him in little things. There the motive can be only supernatural; in big things the motive may be sheer self-seeking. This view means an end to the deliberate search for self-satisfaction in God's service. It means that we realise that it is God Who is to be satisfied. "*I always do the things that please Him,*" (*John. viii,* 29). It means fighting against that attitude which, instead of trying to please God, is ever striving to please self without displeasing God. The cause of the mediocrity that is sometimes found in our spiritual life is to be found in our failure in little things, in the search for our own satisfaction, in our reluctance to detach ourselves from our own pet projects—in a word, our rejection of the Cross.

There it is. We must take up our cross daily. No service or success in the ministry of souls will exempt us from that Divinely imposed task. If we are men of faith and have the mind of Christ, we shall readily believe that we probably do more for souls when on the cross of frustration, than when we are on the Thabor of sensible success. No one can question our Lord's zeal for souls; yet He spent thirty years in obscurity in Egypt and Nazareth and let His active life be cut short by the shameful Crucifixion. That very Cross was St. Paul's only glory and only hope. He died daily to himself, glorying in his infirmities, that the power of Christ might dwell in him. For the Cross is a Tree of Life to all who embrace it willingly. The ideal priest is one in whom Christ lives and who acts for Christ in others, and for God in Christ; we "deny" ourselves only in order that Christ may live in us. There can be no greater fruit of our lives than Christ— for He is all. Let us sum it all up in two quotations: *"In what then doth the progress and perfection of a man consist? In offering thyself with thy whole heart to the Divine will, not seeking the things that are thine either in little or great, in time or eternity,"* (Imitation, Book III). And our Lord's own exhortation says everything: *"If any man will come after Me, let him deny himself, and take up his cross and follow Me. For he that will save his life will lose it; and he that shall lose his life for My sake shall find it,"* (Matt. xvi: 24, 25).— For He is the Way, the Truth, the Life: He is ALL.

E

THE PRIEST AND RECREATION

LIVING IN AN AGE of which the passionate pursuit of pleasure is characteristic, the secular priest may fall into one of two opposite errors. He may drift with the tide and seek pleasure as an end in itself with ardent regularity, or he may reject it altogether as incompatible with a true spiritual life. That the first error is a serious one, is obvious. That the second, too, has its dangers is a lesson of experience. Every human being needs some relaxation and some pleasure. A man may find most of his pleasure in his work, but even then he must change his occupation occasionally; otherwise he goes stale and becomes inefficient. Some recreation is necessary.

But there is a great difference between using pleasure to achieve proper and efficient living, and using life to achieve mere pleasure. The ideal thing would be to have such a degree of detachment that one could use pleasure just in the right measure that is necessary for the efficiency of one's particular work, and could then turn away from it without regret. A priest should be master of his pleasures, never their slave. When he is their master, those pleasures which do not involve sin or scandal can be integrated into his spiritual life. They can, in fact, be used to make us better priests and Christians. But to do so is not always easy.

To come to details, let us take the use of tobacco as an example. In this, as in kindred matters, much depends on local customs and standards. What is considered as shocking in one place is regarded as quite natural in another. For our own part, we cannot accept the view that there is not a natural and a normal use for all such things, but we cannot deny that their use often develops into an abuse. It is true, too, that even their natural use may seem opposed to the spirit of mortification that one would expect in a priest. But, first things first! It is far more important for a priest to curb his temper than to curb his taste for tobacco. One single outbreak of temper in the confessional, or even elsewhere may cause the loss of a soul whom Christ died to save. If a cigar in the evening will remove that danger and soothe a man's irritation, is he not justified in using it? It is quite another thing if the priest becomes enslaved by tobacco.

But temperance can be exercised in the control of these matters, and quite a fair degree of mortification can be called for in keeping one's tobacco consumption down to a proper limit. Perhaps we speak less wisely, but we are haunted by the spectre of a priest, highly mortified in all things else, but with a temper that makes it impossible to approach him, or with a pride of his own self-control that vitiates the whole of it. If we start with the rule: *ne quid nimis,* time and prayer may bring us the grace to achieve a more complete renunciation.

Some may ask—why not start with complete renunciation of all such pleasures ? Well, we grant that the ideal would be such a degree of mortification in which one's real recreation would be found in prayer and in the things of the spirit. But we are dealing with human nature and with men who are not yet saints. We must remember their weakness. Every priest who has sat for hours in the confessional, trying to keep his temper, trying to dispose obstinate sinners, trying to convince the doubting, trying to be kind to the insolent, trying to comfort those who are in trouble, trying to forget all the filth he hears, will realize the benefit of anything that will take him out of himself for a couple of hours. A man who has to be continually ready to improvise answers to questions on all sorts of topics, to meet all sorts of arguments, to find new ideas for a weekly sermon, or—what is still harder—to find new ways of putting old ideas across, must get some relaxation unless he be a mystic of a high order. If he does not get some chance to relax, the strain may have serious effects. And eventually a form of escapism may develop which leads to something far more serious than mere amusement. Even if things do not go so far, one may find one's spiritual life and exercises becoming tepid and even distasteful, simply because of that fatigue and lack of energy which can be such an obstacle to a sound spiritual life. To put it bluntly, the smooth running of an engine calls for a safety valve on the boiler, and if one must blow off steam, it is far better to do so through the legitimate valve than to wait for an explosion!

Some relaxation, then, is necessary, but there must be limits to its quantity and its quality. The modern craze for the cinema has not left the ranks of the clergy untouched.

Where such shows are not banned to them by legislation or by the danger of scandal, the man who makes occasional use of them to escape from his worries, to get an idea of what sort of food his flock is feeding on, to ease his mind by genuine comedy or to gratify a genuine artistic interest, can hardly be blamed. It is quite another matter when a priest becomes so much enslaved to the craze, or so devoted a follower of certain stars, that he simply *must* see a show twice or thrice weekly. There is here, first of all, an inordinate attachment that can be an obstacle to a proper spiritual life. We are far from the *idem velle, idem nolle* that should be our motto. But there is further the fact that the cinema—perhaps undesignedly, but none the less definitely— is, taken as a whole, propaganda for paganism. We are not now speaking of indecency or of gross immorality. We have rather in mind the effect produced by the quiet insistence on the struggle—often unscrupulous—for a materially happy ending with absolutely no reference to God. Virtue, if any, is just natural virtue. The supernatural is left out; and if the repeated achievement of happiness without it has any lesson is it not this—that the supernatural is quite unnecessary ? Even for a priest, constant exposure to such propaganda is not without its dangers. Further, the usual theme of boy-meets-girl, is hardly the best help to celibate living—except, perhaps, for the cynical. And even where there is no indecency, the constant "glamourization" of woman is not calculated to produce a quiet and clean imagination in the celibate beholder. For the casual visitor whose spiritual life is vigorous and well-rooted, these things may produce a healthy reaction. But the regular fan can easily be swept slowly along by the insistent pull of the quiet constant tide. The casual visitor may profit, too, by the sheer passivity of the pleasure. For him, it may be a badly needed relaxation of tension. But the regular devotee is developing a very bad habit of handing over control of his emotions and his mind to—well, perhaps he knows to whom. He is also letting his own personal power of amusing himself atrophy. It is in this inducement of passivity of mind and will that, in our view, lies one of the greatest dangers of the cinema. "Bread and circuses" symptomize the beginning of the degenerate end.

Apart from all that, a priest lets himself down in a very real sense when he just must go to the cinema two or three times a week. Movie standards, movie ideals, movie performances are governed by the box-office, which is really the voice of the mob. The film director must play to the lowest common factor of the crowd. If that is the appeal which captivates the priest—one may well ask, who is he to lead men to better things? Even if the priest is still above that low level, he will soon be dragged down to it. Good taste in natural things is something which no priest can afford to neglect, even if it be only as a bulwark for the preservation of his spiritual tastes, or as a foundation for their development. Now, of all forms of entertainment, few fall lower than the level of the cinema where taste is concerned.

Mutatis mutandis, much of what we have said might be applied to some forms of light reading. However, there can be a great difference. There are works of fiction—even lighter fiction—that can be integrated into the spiritual life of a priest. They may help him to understand his flock, they may start him thinking and give him ideas for sermons, they may distract him from the burden of temptation or of worry long enough to give him time to get his second wind. But they can also be a snare, wasting his time, filling his mind with worldly thoughts, pandering to his less respectable emotions or spoiling his taste for serious reading. Here, too, it is a question of use and abuse.

In fact, there is nothing to be gained by going into all the forms of recreation. Not everyone will agree even with what we have written. Let us then state our principle: In all these things we presume that a priest daily attends to the essentials of his spiritual life—his spiritual reading, his reflection, and his private prayer. We assume that he says Mass daily with some sense of the meaning for his own life of the sacrificial act which he performs. We assume, in fact, that he is a spiritual man, a man of Christ, who is trying to abide in the Vine. Presupposing all that, we are prepared to set the limits of possible recreation fairly widely, relying on the spiritual tastes of the priest to induce him to pick his path carefully within those limits. And while we would exclude no form of recreation that can be prudently and becomingly used by the priest, we have the hope that his growing intimacy with Our Lord, and sharing of His Spirit will lead him to turn away from these make-believe pleasures of man to the joys of Christ's company, somewhat in the same way as a growing taste in art or music or literature makes a man impatient and intolerant of the sham and shoddiness of all that is cheap, superficial, and mean.

Others would prefer to set the limits to a priest's play as closely as possible from the very beginning. We cannot deny that the view has its "probability," and we would not care to undertake the responsibility of opposing it. Yet we cannot but feel that bonds that are set too tight are apt to snap—that too many "dont's" will tend to make a man intolerant of all limitations. The English-speaking world is shot through with a Puritanism that at times tends to colour even Catholic practice. It can produce a tendency to Phariseeism and to that pride that is such an obstacle to true holiness. Liberty of spirit is a necessary element for true spiritual development. Different men need different medicines, and recreation is a medicine. But our liberty must not be used to the scandal of our neighbour. Even if all things are lawful, not all are expedient. Even here, St. Paul has his message for us: "*Take heed lest your liberty become a stumbling-block to the weak,*" (I Cor. viii: 9).

In this chapter we are dealing with recreation quite independently of the question of clerical mortification. That will form the subject of a separate chapter. And there are two important forms of recreation to which we can only allude. Reading—in the sense of the study of some interesting subject—is one. Not everyone has a taste for such reading, but it is well worth trying to cultivate it. History, biography, science, mathematics, have often been a safe and healthy refuge for many a tired priest. Physical exercise is the other. It is a pity that there are not more facilities for such exercise for priests. Twenty minutes' vigorous exercise, especially if it can be taken in the open air, can do wonders to knit up the ravelled sleeve of care, to relieve irritation and to get rid of depression. Manual labour plays such an integral part in the life of a contemplative monk that we may be forgiven for dropping a hint as to its spiritual value for the clergy, where it is possible. Many a priest owes much of his vitality, spiritual as well as corporal, to his garden.

So much depends on local conditions that it is impossible to descend to details. Our view is that if the priest is careful to nourish his spiritual life and to preserve his intimacy with Our Lord, he may set the limits of the choice of his permissible recreation fairly widely; but he must avoid inordinate attachment and entanglement. In a word he must be truly temperate.

MORTIFICATION

THE CONTINUAL EXHORTATION to mortification which is found throughout the Gospels, and which rings out so insistently from the lips of St. Paul, is a favourite theme with all spiritual writers, ancient and modern. It is one, therefore, which no priest may reject without rashness. It is, of course, possible to argue that individual writers here and there perhaps exaggerate its importance, yet the absolute necessity of some degree of mortification is an unavoidable consequence of the fact that we inherit a fallen nature—a nature in which the lower powers are in revolt against the higher, a nature in which the flesh lusteth against the spirit. If we wish to succeed in preventing those lower powers, which may be collectively designated as concupiscence, from taking over control and making it impossible for us to love God with our whole heart and our whole soul, we must make some provision for the establishment of law and order and for the maintenance of effective government in our own selves.

It is sometimes argued that the life of a diocesan priest who is faithful to the duties of his state and truly zealous in the works of his ministry, already contains all the exercise in self-control and self-denial that is necessary. But St. Paul's zeal and energy in his ministry is beyond all question; yet even he found it necessary to chastise his body and bring it into subjection lest he himself should suffer shipwreck. His example should warn us that the necessary habit of self-denial will not be built up if self-indulgence is only then curbed when the work of the ministry is in question. For unless there is a positive habit of self-control for its own sake and for all that it means in our personal relations with God, self-indulgence will take over command when we are off duty in regard to our ministry. But we are never off duty in regard to our own soul and above all, in regard to God. There must be, therefore, in our daily life some positive "non-utilitarian" acceptance or infliction of discomfort (e.g. in our posture when seated), and some deliberate refusal to yield to the otherwise legitimate demands of self-love (e.g. in the use of food, drink, or tobacco, etc.).

This need not be continual, but it must be frequent enough to establish a habit and also a mortified attitude of mind. There are other and perhaps greater motives for mortification, but even in acting from the highest of them we must never lay aside a prudent discretion and moderation. The decision to impose any mortification upon oneself must also include some decision as to the limit of the imposition; otherwise we shall be very slow even to commence the practice. For our very urge to yield to the prompting of grace will be stifled by the fear that we are letting ourselves in for something that has no limits. Where is it all going to stop ? If we lay aside this particular cigar, shall we ever again be able to smoke with peace of mind ? If we sit up straight in our chair this time, shall we ever be able to relax our muscles with a tranquil conscience ? Consultation with a prudent director can be of great help in dealing with this difficulty. But there are some principles that may aid us to solve our difficulties ourselves. We should always remember that liberty of spirit and peace of mind must be preserved as essential factors in a healthy spiritual life. Anything optional, which interferes with their maintenance, can be tranquilly set aside. Again, apart from the case of mortification imposed by law or duty, one may prudently decide to limit oneself to such voluntary mortifications as can be done cheerfully. If we find ourselves murmuring and saddened at the thought of some optional sacrifice, it is probably better to omit it and to accept the humiliation of being so weak. In this way we could achieve a much more important mortification, namely, the mortification of ourself. But it is essential that we do not omit interior mortification. We must carry our mortification into the realm of our thoughts. Day-dreaming, reveries, memories, and anticipations, should be carefully controlled. Of course, a too rigid control of the imagination could be dangerous, for it could easily lead to a reaction in which we would find ourselves carried to the other extreme; but a gentle, prudent watchfulness over the workings of our memory and our imagination is essential for a sound spiritual life. To sum it up in another way: No athlete can run a race unless he trains beforehand; no boxer can reach even the end of the first round unless he has prepared himself by training. So, too, no man can say "no" to himself under temptation unless he trains himself in self-denial. Therefore the Christian must get into training. And he must get into training even in his thoughts, for no man who always says "yes" in his thoughts, will be able to say "no" when it comes to action.

To this need of self-control arising from the effects of original sin on our inherited human nature there are added further motives arising out of our own personal sins. The self-indulgence of sin still further increases the rebellion of the lower powers that original sin initiated, and repeated sins leave behind them bad habits, against which we must make war. But apart from that, we know that God's justice demands reparation, and we know that purgatory is provided as a means of undergoing the temporal punishment due to our sins. We also know that the pains of purgatory, while being incomparably more severe than any sufferings of this life, are nevertheless quite without merit. Prudence, then, would suggest that we choose the easy way of doing our penance here and now, especially since that penance can earn for us a high measure of merit. But the love of God whom we have offended is a much higher motive (and one, incidentally, which can make our penance still more meritorious). In this connection every priest should read the Encyclical of Pius XI on Reparation to the Sacred Heart. The Holy Father exhorts the faithful to make reparation for the sins of men, and he points out that even though the praise and the satisfaction offered up by Christ Himself are alone worthy of God, yet we should add to them our own personal contribution. He even quotes St. Cyprian who affirmed that "the sacrifice of Our Lord is not complete as far as our own sanctification is concerned, unless our offerings and our sacrifices correspond to His Passion," (St. Cyprian: Ep. 63, No. 381).

So far, however, we have been considering the priest as an ordinary Christian. But the priest, and especially the diocesan priest, is something far more than an ordinary person. He is, in fact, something quite extraordinary. He is taken *from among men and is ordained for men in the things that appertain to God, that he may offer up gifts and sacrifices for sins. . . . And therefore he ought, as for the people, so also for himself, to offer for sins.* Now it is true that the principal work of the priest in this matter is to offer up Christ's own sacrifice as contained in the Mass for the sins of the people. But still, even though there be no question of a strict obligation, may we not see a certain fittingness, may we not hear a gentle invitation—a counsel almost—that he should add something of his own to the sacrifice of His Friend and Master? St. Paul found himself urged to fill up in his body the things that are wanting of the sacrifice of Christ for His Body, the Church. Our Lord Himself warned the disciples that a certain sort of devil can only be overcome by prayer and fasting. Can we priests, charged with the salvation of souls, neglect the hints contained in such examples? This is a point upon which we priests might well examine ourselves. When a hard-working priest has checked up on all his duties and activities and can find nothing wrong, when he thinks he has tried all the known ways of tackling the problems of his parish, it is easy for him to persuade himself that if there is anything wrong in the parish, it is not *his fault* —there is nothing more he can do about it. He has tried every form of direct action, but men's hearts are still unchanged. When we reach such an *impasse*, it would be well before disowning all responsibility for the situation, to consider the question of vicarious penance and reparation.

Prayer should be the foundation of our ministry; and our "fasting"—which here stands for all penitential work— might well be the crown of it. It would seem that there are special graces that will not be given to souls unless someone pays a special price for them in penance and suffering. Does not Pius XII write: *"The salvation of many depends on the prayers and the voluntary penances which the members of the mystical Body of Jesus Christ offer for this intention"?* (cf. Encycl. *Mystici Corporis*). Now, we are priests. We represent God before the people, but we also represent the people before God. If then there is need for some special impetration and reparation on their behalf to obtain the grace of their conversion, who is more obviously indicated for the work than we ourselves? At least, until we have tried this way of converting souls, we have no right to say: "There's nothing more I can do about it!"

It is true that there are specially chosen victim-souls whose prayers and sufferings do much to bring down the showers of divine grace. And there are also the contemplative orders whose role in this matter may be gauged from the words of Pius XI, when he urged the establishment of such communities in the mission field, even though it meant immobilizing a number of urgently needed priests. He wrote to the Carthusians: "*It is easy to understand how they who arduously fulfil the duty of prayer and penance contribute much more to the increase of the Church and the welfare of mankind than those who labour in the tilling of the Master's field. For unless the former drew down from heaven a shower of divine graces to water the field that is being tilled, the evangelical labourers would indeed reap from their toil a more scanty crop.*" (Apost. Const. *Umbratilem*, A.A.S. 15.10.24). It is not in order to glorify the contemplative religious at the expense of the diocesan clergy that we invoke this principle here. Quite the contrary, in fact! We quote it, first of all, to warn the diocesan priest that if he does not make the interior work of prayer and penance the mainspring of his apostolic labours, he runs the risk of finding that most of the merit for his successes has been appropriated by somebody else.

But we wish to go further. It is our view that the diocesan priest, should combine together in his own life, the functions of both the active life and the contemplative life. He should stand out above the members of the religious orders as the whole above the part, summing up and including in his own life, as Christ did, the life and activities of each and all. It is indeed a high vocation. But the priesthood should be the highest of all vocations. By his office the priest is called on to *be* perfect; the religious, as such, is only called to *tend* to perfection. And where there is a divine call, there is also the necessary divine grace. *Omnia possum in eo qui me confortat.* There is yet another point of view. We all know how difficult it is to maintain an intimate friendship with one whose outlook, on matters of principle, is different from our own. Indeed we have often used this argument to dissuade the faithful from mixed marriages; for if the two parties go their separate ways on Sunday, if their standards of conduct are at variance, if their motives for action and their views of their final destiny are different, they can never truly share one another's life. Even easy unforced conversation is almost impossible—there are so many topics that must not be mentioned.

Now the priest is the chosen friend of Jesus, and his life must be one of intimate friendship with Him and a complete sharing of His life and work. But the whole life of Christ is characterized by the Cross. Self-indulgence never ruled a single moment of it. Now, how can a man who rejects the Cross and who will not hear of any interference with his self-indulgence, live and work in intimate friendship with Jesus? It is quite impossible! And we have Christ's own warning about it. Such a priest is really in a miserable position. He has all the obligations of the priesthood but few, if any, of its real joys. For, of course, it is in that familiar friendship and constant companionship with the Master that a priest should find his greatest solace and joy. The unmortified priest has none of that joy. It is even difficult for him to look forward to the joys of heaven, for he can see *them* only by faith, and he must dim the light of his faith if he is to remain blind to the lesson of the Cross. As a result he plunges into activity in search of human applause and the satisfaction of achievement. But even if he is successful therein, the thrill soon palls and he is forced to seek lower but more intoxicating joys to satisfy his needs and to deaden his conscience. The danger and misery of his position are only too clear. So, thank God, is its remedy.

Much more could be said on this point, but there is no room for it here; yet we cannot leave the subject of clerical mortification without a few words of warning. The safest mortifications are those which others inflict upon us. The most dangerous are those which increase our pride. It is far healthier to yield to a legitimate desire, admitting how unmortified we are, than to feed one's self-love by the pride of self-control. For the man who prides himself on not being like the rest of men is far from being truly mortified. Quite the contrary! His very success in mortification of one sort has only resulted in a much more objectionable self-indulgence of another sort. Physical mortification that co-exists with temper, "touchiness," and impatience, is always open to suspicion. So also are the mortifications of the man who chastises himself but will tolerate no inconvenience or discomfort caused by others, even when the infliction is quite involuntary on their part. In the infliction of positive pain on one's ownself, and to a lesser degree, in its endurance, great caution is necessary. Modern psychology has revealed to us the possible motives and sources of such actions. Unusual or severe physical penances should never be practised without the advice and continual supervision of a competent director. At the first sign of growing pride or impatience or obstinacy, they should be dropped.

The humble and patient acceptance of all that God's will sends us is the best of all mortifications. If we are truly mortified, we shall at least try to accept rudeness, derision, and contempt, in a spirit of meekness. This is an aspect of mortification that is often overlooked. Finally we must view mortification in its proper perspective. The writers of certain periods use terms of contempt and hatred for the body and for self that seem somewhat exaggerated. Whether in doing so they are somewhat influenced by traces of Jansenism we leave to more competent judges. To our mind the proper approach to mortification is not so much in a spirit of hatred of self, as of love of Christ.

We are members of Christ's Mystical Body. We have received life from Him in Baptism. We deny ourselves only to "assert" Him. We mortify our own self that He may the more freely and the more fully live in us. Mortification, then, even from its most elementary stages, is a quest for, and a development of, union with Christ. When one adds to it a spirit of reparation and tries to share in the work of winning grace for souls, one is entering into a very close partnership with our Friend and Saviour. There are many joys in the spiritual life, but it would seem that the greatest of them all is the joy that is found by generous acceptance of suffering and a prudent generosity in doing penance, for by that, one not only follows Christ but even attains to the fellowship of His sufferings and tastes all the sweetness of perfect friendship with Jesus.

DETACHMENT

THAT CALVINISTIC SPIRIT which sought material success as a sign of spiritual salvation still survives in the English-speaking world as a tendency to regard wealth as a mark and a measure of "respectablity" and to despise poverty as a token of failure. Even Catholics are often found to be infected with the outlook, and the clergy are not always free from the general infection. It is a charge constantly levelled against the clergy by their enemies that they are avaricious: would to God that the charge were always unfounded! Even in our time, there is truth in the following lament of the Council of Milan: "How many priests there are, otherwise, good, modest, of upright life, given to study, exemplary, whom this cursed penuriousness and avarice renders objects of hatred before God and man?"

To appreciate the danger there is in this matter for all of us, let us consider the motives that may lead to this tendency to avarice. The majority of those ordained priests in the English-speaking world were, until the present generation, the offspring of families who had been reduced to beggary and comparative ignorance by penal legislation and had been socially despised as a sort of "white trash." When emancipation came, they tried to fight their way back to "respectability" against many external obstacles as well as a fearful interior inferiority complex. In a society where wealth and material success was the criterion of social standing, it is no wonder that many Catholics pursued material gain with a zeal and avidity that were somewhat inordinate. Many priests inherited this outlook and were unconsciously animated by such a spirit after they were ordained. Their sense of inferiority made them seek to establish themselves in "solid respectablity" by the acquisition of a full purse. Such a policy almost seemed part of their duty to their religion, their priesthood, and their family. This tendency finds further food in the fact that many priests reached the altar only at the cost of considerable sacrifices by their immediate relations. Their vocation involved not only a "*lucrum cessans*" for their relatives through the loss of a son in whom they would find a financial and social asset, but also a considerable outlay. It is natural that such men might feel constrained to do something to make up that loss, and so tend to seek riches. But even if these causes are not operative in every case, there are others that may be. We all know the tendency of the man with an inferiority complex to strive to compensate his low estimate of himself by the acquisition of wealth, of property, or of remarkable things. Men tend to build themselves up in this way by increasing their possessions. Closely connected with this outlook, is the desire to be a generous host. Lavish hospitality is not always animated by sheer altruism; there is a strong strain of pride in it. It may even be the result of a lack of moral courage which makes us afraid of not being as good as our neighbour.

There are many other motives that can lead a priest to seek riches, but we can nearly always trace back the beginnings of our inordinate desire for money to a desire to build ourself up. There is a lack of true self-denial at the root of it. We are not living-up (or should one say, "dying-up ?") to the full meaning of our sacrificial statement made by saying Mass. Unlike our Master, we have not "delivered ourselves." We want to increase whereas He must increase, we must decrease. But our pursuit of money is not always for ourself; it is for our church, for this or that object in the parish, or perhaps for charity! Perhaps it is! But perhaps it is also for ourself! The tendency towards "self-increase" can masquerade under many such forms. When a pastor proudly shows people around "his" church, or tells of the collection toward "his" fund for some special object, one cannot help wondering sometimes whether the accent is not rather on the "his" than on the church. Let it be granted that parochial finance is always a pressing problem and often calls for energetic action. Yet we must be careful that the pursuit for money for the sake of our flock is not used as a subtle means of self-seeking and "self-development." Because there are so many motives which can lead a priest to pursue money, and so many ways in which he could secretly, as it were, satisfy this passion, it is necessary that a priest should take up a very decisive attitude in the matter—all the more so, since it is the one vice from which time does not deliver us. It rather feeds upon the years. As St. Gregory says, "All vices wane as man ages except avarice alone, which never ages."

Life-long vigilance and decisive effort, therefore, are demanded if our ministry and our souls are not to be ruined by a worship of the golden calf. In fact, even though priestly "penury" is not on a par with priestly chastity, yet we would say that a priest should be just as definite and as watchful in renouncing material gain and personal aggrandizement as he is in renouncing marriage. For the quest of gold can ruin his ministry as well as his own soul. People will far more readily forgive other weaknesses of human nature in a priest than this one. As the Council of Milan said, it makes a priest "hateful to God and man." And every-day experience proves it. One has only to hear the comments made on the attitude adopted by some pastors in collecting their due contribution from their flock to realise how true it is. And, in passing, might we utter a plea for some circumspection and Christian reserve on this point. We grant the difficulty of keeping up the income of the parish clergy at its proper level, but surely personal abuse of the unsatisfactory contributor is neither congruous nor Christian! Untold harm can be done in this matter.

The whole question is of special urgency to-day, when there is a world-wide organization attacking not merely the privileges of wealth but even the possession of property in any form, and when that organization is animated by such a hatred of God and of God's ministers that it will lose no chance of exposing every real weakness and every real inconsistency, and will seek for every appearance of such things as a pretext for slinging mud and as a help to make it stick. We, ourselves, may make distinctions between counsels and precepts, between Apostolic times and the present day; the enemy will hardly be so considerate. We must then take care "that our ministry be not blamed."

It is true that a priest has not taken a vow of poverty. But he has been given a divine exhortation and a divine assurance with regard to detachment from worldy goods. *Be not solicitous. . . . Your Father knoweth you have need of these things. Seek ye therefore first the Kingdom of God and His justice, and all these things shall be added to you,* (Matt. vi, 25-33). The important point here is not that we are to be poor, but that

F

we are not to be solicitous—we are not to *seek after* these
things. St. Thomas gives us a principle that may help, when
he says that poverty is praise-worthy only in so far as it
liberates us from solicitude; so that *quanto modus vivendi in
paupertate minorem sollicitudinem exigit, tanto paupertas   est
laudabilior, non autem quanto paupertas fuerit major,* (Contra
Gent. iii, 133).

A priest needs money for the proper discharge of his
functions. He must feed himself, he must clothe himself
decently, he must have a proper library, he must have
sufficient recreation, he must have a due measure of comfort.
He must be sufficiently independent of the rich to be able
to speak and act freely; he must have a sufficient feeling of
security to avoid the distraction of solicitude. But there is
no need that his radio set should be the very last word;
there is no need that his car should be the latest or the most
expensive model; there is no need that his library should be
famous for its first editions or that the walls of his rooms
should rival an art gallery. Even in the use of gold, there is
a golden mean! The fundamental reason for our tendency
to pass beyond that mean is a lack of faith. That was the
reproach made by Our Lord to His disciples. Our mistake
is that we will not trust Him. His promises are not good
enough for us. The opinion and the example of our fellow-
men count too much with us. We feel we must be able to
buy all that we want. We must be as good as our neighbour.
We must be beholden to no man. We must make provision
for every possible future eventuality. God's promises, God's
providence, God Himself, are not enough for us! That may
seem rather strong, but when one considers the repeated
and explicit teaching of Our Lord and His own example,
when one recalls all the criticism one hears of both priests
and religious on this point, such vigorous statements may be
excused. After all, it really is our faith that is wanting. If
we really believed Our Lord, we should pray for our daily
bread and leave all the rest to Our Heavenly Father Who
looks after the lilies of the field and the birds of the air, Who
provides for the just and the unjust, and Who knows we
have need of all these things.

Another factor is our failure to live up to the sacrificial
promises which we make to God every morning by offering

sacrifice. If we really mean all that the sacrifice of Christ offered in the Mass means, then we should try to spend our lives in self-surrender to God. Like Christ we should continually try to deliver ourselves—to empty ourselves. The quest of worldly wealth is hardly compatible with that self-surrender. Even at the risk of seeming extreme, we would say that in some ways, a priest given to avarice could hardly be in a worse position. There are worse vices—but they are humiliating ones. Greed, however, hardens a man's heart, closes his eyes to the things of the next world and to the supernatural, and feeds his pride at the same time. To this is added a blindness that makes a cure still more difficult, for the avid quest for gold is so much in harmony with the spirit of society and of the times that, so far from being clearly wrong, it can even seem quite reasonable and praiseworthy. Yet it is utterly incompatible with what Our Lord taught His Apostles. He set them the example of the Good Shepherd who "giveth his life for his sheep". . . *But the hireling flieth because he is a hireling and hath no care for his sheep*, (John x, 13). That text alone would be sufficient condemnation of the pastor who seeks personal gain in his ministry. But there are even stronger exhortations. *Everyone of you that doth not renounce all that he possesseth cannot be my disciple!* (Luke, xiv, 34). Of course that very definite principle must not be taken without the corresponding assurance: *Everyone that hath left house or lands for My name's sake, shall receive a hundredfold in this life, and shall possess life everlasting.* (cf. Matt. xix, 29). But the very fact that Our Lord has given us such a magnificent reassurance only makes our renouncement all the more urgent. In regard to these statements of Our Lord's, it might be well for us to ask ourselves—for surely they were addressed to us priests before anyone else—do we really believe what Our Lord says therein, and if we do, how can we say that we have faith if we are still solicitous?

Here then is matter for courageous consideration and for a practical decision. Not merely is the health of our own soul involved, but the whole work of our ministry. For nothing so sterilizes our ministry as avarice. It gives the lie to our preaching, since we ourselves contradict the whole burden of the Gospel. How can a man known to be a

worldling hope to persuade people to live for another
world ? How can a man exhort his congregation to be
generous to the poor and to the parish, if they know he himself is so attached to his wealth ? How can the poor and
the afflicted accept exhortations to patience and resignation
from a man who dreads financial insufficiency and flies from
all discomfort? Each one of us will have to work out his
own counter-attack on the enemy, but for all, the first point
is detachment. We must not be solicitous. The second
point is to avoid being excessively well-off. It should be
possible for a priest, by comparing notes with his fellow
clergy, to decide what is a reasonable income for a man in
his position. If he finds his income passing this figure, might
we suggest that he appoint himself an income-tax officer,
and that he levy an excess profits tax by putting a heavy
super-tax (50 per cent. would not be too much!) on all that
he receive above this agreed figure ? The "tax" could be
distributed in parochial charity, or it would find a very
fitting application in helping the education of students for
the priesthood. That is only a suggestion. But one cannot
read the Gospel without realizing that something positive
must be done about our attitude to money. *Blessed indeed
is the man who hath not gone after gold, nor put his trust in money
nor in treasures*, (cf. Eccles. xxxi, 8). Blessed is he indeed for
only those who have renounced all solicitude and cast their
burden on the Lord, have really discovered how wonderful
is the providence of God. God is indeed the Father of the
poor, and there is no limit to His thoughtfulness and His
solicitude for those who put all their hope in Him.

The ecstacies of the saints have all a common origin in
a perception of the extraordinary fullness of truth in the
words: My God and My All! For one who puts his hope in
money, Christ is not enough; but for one who puts all his
hope in Christ, Christ is indeed All. Blessed indeed is such
a one, for the Father of the poor Who knoweth he hath need
of "all these things" will add them all unto him, rendering
him a hundredfold in this life and eternal life hereafter,
manifesting to him, even now, the tremendous depth of
truth in the words: "God will provide."!

CELIBACY

IT IS NOT EASY to treat in print of the problems connected with clerical celibacy. They are all rather delicate, and may often depend upon the variations of personal temperament. But it is essential that every priest should adopt the right and necessary outlook in this matter. If he regards himself as one who is consecrated and offered up to God daily in his Mass, his spirit of sacrifice and renunciation will soon produce that attitude required. A priest has renounced, definitely and permanently, a certain type of sense pleasure obtained in marriage. In doing so he has renounced the satisfaction of what is one of the strongest and most insidious of the human passions, and he lives in a world which seems almost expressly organized to provoke that passion. Consequently no mere negative and passive attitude is sufficient. He must at least look as far as his outer defences. And above all he must never take his chastity for granted. He dare not for a moment forget that he is a man—that the Roman collar has in no way removed the inherited tendencies of the flesh— that there is nothing fire-proof or asbestos-like about the cassock. He has declared war on an enemy whose strongest division is its fifth column already securely entrenched within his own camp. But the priest has gone further. In addition to renouncing the satisfaction of his passions, he has also renounced a much higher type of pleasure—the companionship, the sympathy, the understanding, the romance, the consolation, which arise from loving and being loved in marriage. These two things may be distinct, but they are closely connected; and it is because of failure to remember the second renunciation and all that it implies, that more than one unfortunate man has fallen in regard to the first one. In fact the really dangerous assaults on clerical chastity are usually quite indirect and our defence policy must be planned with that in mind.

The first point of capital importance is: *Never to take one's chastity for granted.* The man who upon hearing of someone's fall, exclaims "That could never happen to me!" is in proximate danger of a catastrophe. There are men whose natural passions are weak and who do not experience any

83

strong temptation, but they are in the minority. Most men
must pray daily to God with St. Augustine: *Da mihi castitatem—*
but, unlike him, they must add: *Modo, Domine.* And the Book
of Wisdom tells us: *As I knew I could not otherwise be continent,
except God gave it. . . . I went to the Lord and besought Him,*
(Wisdom viii: 21). The sense of our weakness and our constant need for God's help can be a foundation of a most
precious union with Jesus Christ, Who comes to save us.
With St. Paul we can gain say: *Libenter gloriabor in infirmi-
tatibus meis, ut inhabitet in me virtus Christi,* (II. Cor. xii, 9). But
our prayer will not be sincere unless we do our own part. We
must avoid those things which are for us a source of danger.
Custody of the eyes is an age-old prescription which has not
lost its efficacy. But it must be used with prudence. The real
incitement to passion is not so much in the exterior object
as it is in its real self, but as it is elaborated by the imagination. If the temptation comes from within, starting in the
imagination, the sight of the reality may destroy its glamour.
So, too, when one has just caught a passing and incomplete
glance of some attractive object, a full and complete look
may prevent the imagination elaborating a picture of exaggerated glamour and seductive power. One priest, a religious, who had frequently to meet women on committees,
etc., found all such interviews a source of great trouble and
temptation. He sought advice on the matter, and was asked
whether he looked at the women. "Of course not—I keep
my eyes cast down!" "Well, Father," was the reply, "for
the next two weeks take a comprehensive look at each
woman you speak to, and I'll be responsible for any evil that
may ensue!" In a week the priest was cured. But custody of
the eyes is essential; and men have only themselves to blame
if they imprudently feed their imagination on movies and
magazine advertisements. There is need, too, for interior
mortification of the memory and of the imagination, which
should be exercised even before conscience warns one of sin.

   Then there is the whole difficult question of our relations
with women. Let us grant the possibility that modern
life and customs may render the safeguards found
in many authors somewhat extreme. *Numquam solus cum
sola! Sit sermo brevis et durus,* etc. For all that, more than
one poor man only realized their value and importance

after his neglect of them had led to a crash. Still, there is room for a prudent discretion in accepting the details of such safeguards. Exaggeration may defeat their purpose by making even sound and necessary precautions seem ridiculous. If we recognize that any friendship with a woman can be dangerous, we shall tend to be on our guard. Much, of course, depends upon particular circumstances. Friends we have known intimately from boyhood cannot be classed quite indiscriminately with those met after ordination. Very special circumstances excepted, a new intimate friendship formed with a woman after ordination, should be regarded with great suspicion, if not for what it already is, at least for what it may become. Human nature is human nature. Men and women have a natural attraction for one another. They find in each other a natural complement, satisfying a need that may sometimes be keenly felt. God himself told us that it is not good for man to be alone. Unless a priest make God his Friend and Partner, human nature may become imperious in its demands. It is dangerous to think that mental intimacy has no connection with physical intimacy. There is a co-ordination of mind and body that even the Liturgy recognises. Friendship may start in a common intellectual or cultural interest; it may even begin on a very high spiritual plane. But it may not be easy to keep it within such limits. There are various influences that may provoke its deterioration. Jealousy is one. Vanity is another. Even curiosity may lead to trouble. A desire not be outdone by somebody else, an urge to show what one could do if one really tried, an itch to know whether the other's indifference is feigned or real—such feelings have more than once led to disaster. Where a considerable degree of affection has arisen, there is a great danger for one who has mistaken fastidiousness for chastity. For what formerly appeared nasty, now presents itself in quite a new and alluring light and will only be avoided by a very definite virtue of real chastity.

Sometimes the trouble begins in an attempt to give consolation. The principle that consolation which cannot be given with mere words should not be given by a priest is quite sound, and should always be followed even in bona-fide cases. But not all cases are quite bona-fide. In an age when "experience" has tarnished the escutcheon of many men, there is something about clerical continency that may have an appeal for women, even for women with ideals. This approach may be quite insidious and their real motive may be quite unperceived even by themselves. To the less idealistic, the charm of forbidden fruit may be an allure; and there is no end to the motives that make some women hunt for scalps, counting the clerical scalp as a special trophy. It is not necessary to detail the catalogue. No priest who knows the world can fail to see the need for perpetual vigilance. He has a special duty to avoid exciting desires that cannot be satisfied, in others as well as in himself. One great safeguard in all these matters is absolute candour with an understanding confessor who is not afraid or unable to say what he thinks. In particular, let no man think he is a theologian in his own case when it comes to estimating the gravity of matter. It is true that for those acquainted with the attitude of modern urban civilization, the judgments of some theologians as to what is *graviter excitans* and what is not, may seem too strict. Yet an interested party can become quite an adept at building up a probable opinion on the benign side. Soon one theologian constitutes a sound probable opinion. Then mere *obiter dicta* are taken as general principles. Then new rules of interpretation as to "what he really means" are evolved. The different sorts of *delectatio* are sorted out with a nicety that is extreme; grave matter becomes light; light matter becomes an imperfection; and soon all degrees of wrong are swept away by "excusing causes." Only the experienced confessor has any notion how a man can fool himself in this matter. That is why we so strongly urge candour with a confessor. Of course, he must be an understanding one. Views that are too rigorous do more harm than good. Their exaggeration is easily perceived, and because of it the whole opinion is discarded instead of the part that is exaggerated. For similar reasons, exaggeration, too, in the prescription of safeguards is also dangerous. But there was another reason behind our previous reference to this point. To our mind it is essential from the very start that there must be no half-heartedness about a priest's renunciation in this matter. It must be wholehearted and complete. It must lead to a willing acceptance of all its necessary consequences, and of all genuinely sound precautions. If those suggested are too extreme or too extensive, one may begin to pick and choose just how far he will observe them, and a beginning is made that may lead to a divided heart, to an incomplete renunciation and an inadequate resolution that may have fatal results.

There are many social activities and recreations that are at least imprudent—if not definitely barred—for a man who has vowed celibacy. Here we would warn the man who finds himself a little sad about these limitations to his activities to examine his resolution in their regard. Is it adequate? Is it whole-hearted? Is it sincere? Does he keep to it even in his imaginings? If he forgets it in his reveries, he may soon forget it in his real life. One great source of limitation to a priest's conduct is the danger of scandal. The opinion is widely held today among non-Catholics that continence is impossible, that the sex appetite will satisfy itself one way or another, and so the modern critic tends to read into even the most innocent actions of a priest, a significance in harmony with his views. It is true, the scandal of the Pharisees can sometimes be despised. But the good name of the ministry has its claims, and the efficacy of our apostolate must be preserved. There is just one other point. Alchoholism is not the only form of escapism to which the nervous temperament may have recourse. There are mild forms of anxiety neuroses, and other psychological conditions, that can occasion severe temptation of another sort. Mental hygiene is of great importance for a priest— even for his virtue; and the service of a sound Catholic psychiatrist should be sought at an early date if there is any tendency to trouble of this sort. In particular, confessors and others who have to deal with such cases, should remember that they nearly all have the origin in a more or less unconscious fear or anxiety. Harsh treatment or threats will only make things worse. Kindness, sympathy, and encouragement are essential in all such cases. But in regard to those who come to us for direction we should remember that it is a well-known fact that personal attachment often lessens considerably a priest's official powers of guidance. He does not seem to have the same grace for his work. And there may be considerable truth in the frequently repeated observation that the bestowal of inordinate affection by a priest on any person brings a blight that is almost a curse. But the real defence, the proper policy, is a whole-hearted search for God and a complete union with Christ. True chastity must find its support in a full and fervent interior life wherein Christ is all in all.

SELF-SACRIFICE

TRADIDIT SEMETIPSUM. This text could be taken as an excellent summing-up of the life and death of Our Lord. It should, at least, be an ideal for the priest, and might well be taken as a constant principle of all his actions and his sufferings and his submissions. And since it was by obedience even to death that Christ delivered Himself, it is by a similar sacrifice of his own will that the priest must follow Him. In previous chapters on humility, on chastity, on detachment from wealth, we have considered some ways in which the ideal of self-"deliverance," of self-sacrifice, can be realized. Under the head of ambition we include all those tendencies to the building up of "self" that appear in so many forms: the quest for self-development, for advancement, for a career, for renown, for popularity, for achievement. The motives that lie at the root of such ambitions are many and varied. The pride of life is strong in all of us. We must make the grade! The natural feeling of inferiority that resulted from our youthfulness makes us seek an assurance of our mature value in successful work, and to this motive there is often added the more morbid driving-power of an inferiority complex, born of a keenly felt resentment of our own limitations. Society, too, by its example, its standards, its judgments, can cause us to adopt its own outlook and to seek a success to which we can point, even if it be only in the privacy of our own thoughts, with satisfaction and pride. Such urges can, of course, lead to energetic work in our ministry, and that work, *ex opere operato* as it were, can be fruitful. But the fruit is not credited to us, and there is a more excellent way of bearing fruit. And such motives of ambition may even destroy the fruitfulness of our work, for one great danger of all such motives and principles of action is their inevitable tendency to develop self-will and to interfere with our practice of obedience.

The man who is determined to seek a "successful" career feels it necessary to take his life into his own hands and fashion it, with foresight and energy, to his purpose. Even if his position is such that he must conform, externally, at least, to the orders of a superior, he still seeks himself and his own will in that service. Even under a superior, there are various ways of getting oneself appointed and "ordered" according to one's own desires. A hint in the right place, a careful piece of flattery, skilful intrigue and wire-pulling, can do much to that end. We can be "difficult" and unsatisfactory when set at an undesirable task; we can make trouble and so force the hand of authority to put us where we want to be. The technique is only too well exemplified in many branches of modern life. Now all such policies are quite opposed to the spirit of priesthood, to the spirit of Christ. We swore obedience to the Bishop at our ordination, and that obedience is something more than a mere avoidance of direct defiance. It is something more, too, than a mere will to obey inside certain limits, outside which we are free to do what we think is our real work and to determine our own activity. Obedience is rather a complete handing-over of ourself, our faculties and our talents to him whom the Holy Ghost has appointed to rule the Church, to be used as it shall seem good to him and to the Holy Ghost. Even though a Bishop be not inspired in commanding, yet we are more than inspired in obeying. For by obeying, we "abide in Christ." And by abiding in Christ, we are made fruitful, quite independently of the nature of the work which we are ordered to do. For our fruitfulness is supernatural, not natural. And there is no other way of bringing forth supernatural fruit than by abiding in Christ by doing His will in charity.

It is quite true that such a life of complete subordination to the appointments and to the policy of another—to say nothing of subordination to the demands of our fellow-men and the force of circumstances—may destroy any hope of our using our best talents in the most successful manner. It may, of course, mean for some men a life of external success, perhaps beyond their merits; but for others—more able perhaps and more brilliant—it may mean a life of uncongenial tasks, performed with little satisfaction and no renown, while their best powers wither for want of the waters of opportunity, and they see someone else applauded for work that they know they themselves could do better. The preacher may have to organize, the organizer may have to teach, the teacher may have to write, the writer may have to serve the sick. Frustration can indeed be written large in the lives of those subject to authority.

To some extent at least such experiences will fall to the lot of every priest, and his eternal destiny and that of many souls may depend on the way he re-acts to it. One can adopt "hedgehog tactics," becoming difficult and even defiant, in the hope of forcing a change. One can perform one's set tasks with a minimum of zeal and energy while devoting oneself to some other work of one's own choice as one's real interest. One can even do worse, and in the spirit of defiance and revolt, plunge into an ever deepening degradation of sin, throwing over the virtue of temperance in one or all of its branches. And such policy is fatal, both for our own life and those of the others who depend on us. (We must never forget that we are "fathers"; we have a family—2,000, it has been said—depending on each of us for bread). And one might say that a man who adopts such an attitude ceases in many ways to be a priest. For every priest is taken from among men and is *ordained for men in the things that appertain to God, that he may offer up gifts and sacrifices for sins*. And here is a man appointed to such a work by the vice-gerent of the Holy Ghost—a man who rebels because he is thereby prevented from living in renown among men, in the things that appertain to himself and to his own glory, refusing to offer up the sacrifice that must be the interior core and principle of all gifts and sacrifices, namely, his own will. Here is a man, a priest by ordination and therefore another Christ. Christ, however, did not His own will, but came to do the will of the Father Who sent Him and emptied Himself taking the form of a servant, becoming obedient unto death, even to the death of the Cross. This man, however, comes to the priesthood to do his own will, not that of the Father Who sends him; he wants to develop himself, to avoid the death of obedience—for it is a death—and to escape the degradation of the cross of failure. That is why we say that such a man ceases to be a priest even though the indelible character is stamped on his soul.

These views may seem extreme. So they are. But the priesthood is an extreme thing. It is in fact the fullness of that very extreme thing—participation in the Divine nature and incorporation in Christ—which takes place at

Baptism. And the reason why so many of us find something unreasonable and unwelcome in this complete submission is because the view we take of our ordination as priests is not extreme enough. If Baptism be a death to self and to sin, and a resurrection to a complete newness of life in Christ— what is the priesthood? Is there anything in common between the life of the man and the life of the priest? Did not Our Lord say that unless a man deny himself and follow in his Master in a daily crucifixion, a daily death, he *cannot* be His disciple? Those are extreme words, terribly extreme! Yet they are spoken categorically by the lips of Infinite Truth. And they refer directly and expressly to us priests. And if we are to put such extreme words into practice, no superficial fufillment is sufficient. We must go down to the root of our self; we must deny our self-will.

To cut short the discussion, let us remember that a priest is a branch of the vine. He must abide in Christ, and Christ must abide in him. Note Our Lord's word "abide." It is not merely at peak points in our ministry that He acts in us. He *abides* in us, and we must *abide* in Him. If we remember that every single fruitful act of our lives, both personally as Christians and ministerially as priests, is the work of grace, we shall realize that it is not only when we consecrate or absolve that Christ takes over our faculties—so to speak. Due proportion being guarded, it may be said that in every act of our priestly lives, the agent is as really Christ as it is when we say: "This is my Body," "I absolve thee. . . .", for it is God who worketh in us both to will and accomplish.

If then the priest is so completely incorporated into Christ and endowed with the power, it is clear that any pursuit of a career, or any attempt to exploit his own talents or his own personality, any quest for renown or reward, is a descent from the sublime to the ridiculous. Compared with the sublime talent of Christ's Spirit and Christ's priesthood and Christ's power that is given to the priest, even the greatest intellect and the greatest of natural gifts are but straw. And the case is worse than ridiculous if one's claim to renown is based on one's supernatural success—for that is robbery from God. We might as well claim personal merit for the power to consecrate the Body of Christ as for any other act of our ministry. What have we that we have not received?

What have we that is ours? What have we that is not
Christ's? We are Christ's, and our life is hid with Him in
God.

It is because we are so completely dependent upon Christ
in our priesthood that obedience is so important for the
priest. Elsewhere we have tried to show that obedience is
the law of the Christian's life in Christ, inasmuch as it makes
us live as members according to the soul of the Mystical
Body Who is the Holy Spirit. If this is true of all members,
how much more true is it of the priest? In fact, so far from
obedience being regarded as unavoidable difficulty in our
work, an unpleasant limitation, an obstacle to be overcome
it should rather be sought and insisted upon as the essential
means to the end that our work may be done in Christ,
that it may be fruitful, that it may be done by Christ
Himself. If we wish to develop and cultivate the life of
Christ in us, it can only be done by acting according to the
will of God as manifested through the recognized channels,
especially through the voice of authority, for this will of
God is the meat that is the food of Christ in our souls.

This consideration may help those whose zeal for success
in their work, even when it is truly apostolic, finds an apparent
hindrance in obedience. Their best plans are turned down,
their initiative is checked, their work is hampered at every
turn. It seems so odd! It is not personal success that they
are seeking, it is the good of souls. Yet the powers-that-be,
seem to be blind to the situation! So much fruit to be brought
forth and gathered if only we could persuade the higher
powers to say: "Go ahead, Father!" Yes, but we must not
forget that when Our Lord told us that abiding in Him is
the one source of our fruitfulness, He added the extraordinary warning that His Father, the husbandman, would
prune the branch so that it might bring forth *more* fruit! This
pruning action is found in all those official limitations to
our activity and zeal. We must then be careful lest our zeal
be the principle of its own frustration.

Much more could be written on the subject. It must here
suffice to draw attention to Our Lord's example. His whole
humanity was completely subordinated to the Holy Spirit;
His human will completely subject to the will of God. He

emptied Himself, laying down all initiative, all use of His own powers. He summed it up Himself: *I am in the Father and the Father in Me. The words I speak to you I speak not of Myself. But the Father who abideth in Me, He doth the works,* (John xiv, 10). There is our model. If the Son of God can so completely deny His own self, empty His own self, deliver His own self— surely we must go and do likewise—surely we must go and die with Him! Actually, if only a priest could summon up the courage to see his whole life as a priest as a "delivering of himself"; if he could see each 'phone call, each visit, each demand on his services or on his time, as an occasion to deliver himself, he would be amazed could he but know the fruitfulness of his life! *Unless the seed falling into the ground die, itself remaineth alone. But if it die, it bringeth forth much fruit,* (John xii: 24, 25). Christ gave life to the world by obedience unto the death of the Cross. We are other Christs. We are called "Father", we are placed to give life to souls. We can only do that by dying to ourselves daily, by renouncing all our own will, by putting on Christ. "Let us go and die with Him."

LAPSUS LINGUAE

TO DISCUSS THE use of speech in connection with the spiritual life would really need a whole book. Any brief discussion of the subject must be inadequate, yet because it is so important, something must be said of it here. The avoidance of all fault in speech calls for consummate perfection: does not St. James say: *If any man offend not in word, the same man is a perfect man,* (James iii, 2)? But for us priests, there is an urgent need of making earnest and continual efforts to tame our tongue, for otherwise our speech will betray not only ourselves but also our ministry. In the first instance we must be scrupulous in regard to truth. A lie is degrading in a layman; in a priest it would be contemptible. But apart from direct lies, there are other ways of offending against the truth—there are exaggerations, there are unwarranted evasions, there are cowardly silences; and against all these we must always be on our guard. We represent God before the people as His ambassadors. We are the mouthpiece of Infinite Truth. In this matter especially, *noblesse oblige.*

Still greater is the need for care in regard to charity and justice. Direct detraction or calumny, of course, would be scandalous in the mouth of a priest; and only a hardened or passion-blind conscience would fail to react quickly to even the beginning of such a sin. Indirect offences of this type, however, are more easily overlooked. The tendency to repeat gossip or rumour for its "news" value, the expression of unfair and unwarranted interpretation of his motives, or even the failure to defend or explain the actions of another, are only some of the many ways in which we can offend indirectly. The inferiority complex that is by no means unknown in the ranks of the clergy, often seeks compensation in some such way. It has been said with great truth that no woman can talk about another woman without giving herself away to those who know how to understand the significance of her comments. Something similar is true of priests, and that is a consideration—though not one of a high order—which may help us to be cautious.

Discretion, of course, should be characteristic of a priest's conversation, yet we all have not the same gift of prudence.

On one point, however, we should be ruthless with ourselves, namely, in regard to keeping absolutely secret all
confidences entrusted to us. And it would be well to carry
our determination in this matter well beyond the boundary
set by the strict obligation. It should, of course, be unnecessary to mention the harm that can be done by repeating
personal comments or criticisms made by others, especially
to the subject of such remarks, yet we priests sometimes
forget the need for reserve in this matter. Humour can be
the salt of speech at times and may help to smooth many
difficulties; but why must so many of us find our fun in a
comment that hurts someone else? Let an unfortunate
assistant make some blunder that any one of us could have
made just as easily, and he becomes the target of many a
painful jest, which he is expected to take in quite good
part. In point of actual fact, such comments, even though
they be jests, are really faults against charity. There is,
however, a great and very important difference between
laughing at a man and laughing *with* him. The latter can
be quite a charitable way of covering up another's blunder,
but the ridicule involved in the former, takes its place with
sarcasm and harsh cynicism as outside the bounds of
priestly conduct.

Clerical humour can also pass proper limits in its subjects.
The impropriety that can sometimes be associated with
genuine humour is not exactly edifying on clerical lips.
However, it would be well to remember that sometimes
such humour is a well-meant safety-valve for the thoughts
that can obsess and depress a man after a long spell of
hearing confessions. It can also be a desperate defence
against temptations. The humour that tends to lessen reverence and regard for sacred things and functions is something
against which we should be on our guard. It is true that
English-speaking folk tend to conceal their feelings and their
devotion by a casual flippancy and careless understatement;
yet this has its dangers when there is question of things to be
known and appreciated only by faith. For example, a due
sense of the awful power and responsibility involved in
giving absolution is always liable to be blunted by manifold
repetition; but if we are in the habit of speaking of our work
as confessors in a jesting manner, that very necessary sense

could easily be lost altogether. There is a happy mean between a prim pomposity and an irreverent indifference that should prevail even when speaking among ourselves. With the laity of course, we must be still more circumspect.

In our contacts with the laity there is danger of another error involving not merely the matter of reverence, but even of moral standards. It is true that we have excellent authority for the policy of being "all things to all men," and every priest should have a ready sympathy and understanding for the weaknesses of human nature. But the priest must never go so far as even in appearance to identify himself with the worldling. There are some priests who, in an honest endeavour to contact souls and lead them to God, lay aside priestly reserve and adopt a manner of speech and behaviour which seems to assert that there is really no difference between the priest and citizen of the world. In his choice of words, of stories, of amusement, in his "broadmindedness" —such a priest adopts the standards of sinful men. This policy may arise from mistaken zeal, but it can also be the result of a desire for popularity, and it may even spring from a dissatisfaction with the limitations of the clerical state. Whatever its motives, such conduct is absolutely fatal. It *may* achieve popularity—it will never induce respect. And it will never make the message which the priest is ordained to deliver, either popular or respected. It is really complete treachery to one's priesthood, and a very bad letting-down of one's self. Quite different from that is the attitude of the priest, who, while retaining his own standard and principles, can understand and sympathise with the difficulties and weaknesses of the worldling and even see matters with his eyes. This in fact should be the aim of every priest. But while doing so, he must never abandon his own position.

On the other hand, there is an affected "edification," an artificial piety of speech and manner, that was sometimes considered proper, but which to-day would only tend to repel souls and to render our message suspect. Exaggerated "earnestness" and all such affectations are foreign to the people of to-day. Sincerity is the characteristic key-note which the sublimity of our office and the outlook of to-day both make essential in our speech. This sincerity will unconsciously arise from a true interior life and familiar friendship with Christ. The fact that we share and maintain Christ's own outlook does not make it necessary for us to be "shocked" or to affect horror when we hear of the sins of men. The attitude of Our Lord to the woman taken in adultery shows us quite a different example. The artificial reactions which are too often to be seen, remind the shrewd observers of the man who "doth protest too much." There may be a personal motive producing them—one not entirely to our credit. Compensation for one's own failings is often the real mainspring of criticism. There are other failings in speech that it would be well for the priest to avoid. Aggressiveness is always objectionable and seldom of any use. The priest who always starts an argument, whose aim is rather to overthrow than to understand, to smash rather than to sympathise, to force rather than to encourage, is not a good shepherd of souls. Cutting remarks, smart answers, unfair arguments, are really opposed to charity as well as to sincerity. It is nearly always a mistake to refuse to admit ignorance—at least if one tries to cover it up by bluff. There are questions that only an expert can answer, difficulties that only a specialist can solve. We need not be afraid to admit our own limitations, and the implication that Catholic theology is a wider subject than can be crammed into the head of one ordinary man is by no means an ineffective argument. Facile, superficial solutions, answering a difficulty by dodging it, can do great damage and lead to serious doubt.

If sincerity is essential for a priest in the use of his tongue, so also is kindness. Nothing was ever lost by being kind and there are many souls whom nothing else but kindness will touch. Kindness is the flower and fruit of charity, and a human counterpart of the divine mercy—which is over all the works of God. It makes a man Christlike, and what is more desirable in a priest than that? There is no great need—and here there is no more space—to extend the catalogue of our failings in speech. The words we have just mentioned, *sincerity* and *kindness*, sum up all that one's speech should be, and they give us a touchstone to detect its defects. What is needed here is some indication of a practical remedy and means which one can use to mend one's ways and to avoid further faults. As usual, our remedy is an attitude of mind, and what we have to say here applies equally to many of the topics previously discussed in former articles—such as, for example obedience. If the priest regards himself as a participator in Christ's Victimhood as well as in His Priesthood, if he offers himself up to God together with Christ the Victim in his daily Mass, and if he endeavours to see in every incident of the day an opportunity for the performance and fulfilment of that oblation, then all else will fall into line. The aim of the priest will be to immolate himself and to accept each divinely-sent agent of immolation. All faults in speech can be traced to an undue assertion of self. The priest must *deliver* himself, not assert himself. That may seem far-fetched and unnecessary, but there is no other way of saving souls. That is how Christ saved the world and we can only follow in His footsteps.

It is true a priest may have to assert his priesthood; then it is Christ he is asserting, not himself. Then there need be no offence in his speech. But all harshness, all lying, all exaggeration, all injustice, all uncharitableness, all criticism, all impatience, all idle gossip, is merely an attempt to put one's self above one's fellows, to make ourselves something, to lower others if we only can raise ourselves, to attract attention or admiration, to be feared if not loved. Self-denial—in the true sense of the word, which is the literal sense—is the remedy for that, and self-denial is merely a negative and unnatural thing unless it comes from "putting on" or "asserting" Christ. In a word, the priest must live the Mass. He owes that to God, he owes it to his flocks, he owes it to himself. There is no other way in which a priest can truly discharge *any* of his sacerdotal obligations. Let us repeat it, a priest must be a victim; a priest, to be a true priest, must live the Mass.

THE CONFESSOR

THERE ARE VERY FEW works of the ministry of a priest in which he can do so much good and so much harm as when hearing confessions. In all his works, a priest must be an *alter Christus*, but hardly ever more so than in the confessional. The Jews themselves in their enmity could not avoid true testimony of the attitude of Christ to sinners: "This man receiveth sinners." This should be the ideal and the motto of every confessor. The qualifications which a priest needs to fulfil this office are many and varied; but if there be any one qualification more urgently needed than the rest, it is that one which makes a priest so Christlike: the virtue of kindness. No one who approached Our Lord to ask His forgiveness was ever received with anything but kindness. This kindness should be our characteristic as confessors. Without it our work will be hampered in every way. The very efficacy of the Sacrament may be frustrated through lack of the necessary dispositions in the penitent if we are not kind. On the other hand kindness is the key to all men's hearts. If anything can dispose the hardest of hearts, it is kindness. Yet, unfortunately, kindness is not always evident in the attitude of many confessors. Some confessors seem to regard the penitent as one who has offended themselves rather than their Divine Master. Others seem to regard it as their chief function to upbraid and humiliate the sinner. And there are many other reactions only too often found in confessors, which seem completely contrary to the example proposed by Our Lord when He spoke of the Good Shepherd searching out the lost sheep and laying it on His shoulders to carry it home—rejoicing.

No one, however, who has sat in a stuffy confessional for any length of time can help having a considerable sympathy for the extravagances of confessors. There are penitents who would try the patience of an archangel. There are those who will do anything except speak up. Others are so reticent and incomplete in their answers that numerous questions are necessary before the confessor can drag out the information necessary to specify the sin. Others will insist on going into long details about venial sins, and glide over matter far more serious. The continual strain to hear, to attend, to guard one's replies, is trying enough. But the circumstances of time and place are often far from propitious to patience. A stuffy box in a stuffy church; street noises breaking in—or perhaps stopping—at the wrong moment; the sometimes unavoidable necessity of getting through as quickly as possible; these and a hundred others can make things very difficult. Fatigue, want of sleep, headache, bodily ills, depression, may add strength to the other enemies of patience. And the wiles of the devil himself, who sees his prey being snatched out of his grasp, cannot be left out of the reckoning. To deal with all these difficulties and to maintain throughout an attitude of patient, calm kindness, a deep interior life is needed. Mere zeal for personal success is not sufficient; such zeal may sometimes even defeat itself. Close union with Our Lord is what He Himself laid down as the only necessary and sufficient condition for fruitful action. Without this union with Christ, a man may succeed as a psychiatrist, or as a temporal counsellor, but no matter how well endowed by nature, he will never succeed as a true confessor—as a successful physician of souls. We cannot too often insist on this principle. Divine union is the only way to achieve fruitful action. The work of the ministry is a supernatural work: it can only be done supernaturally, by a supernatural agency. Natural talents and equipment may play their part as disposing causes, but they must be used supernaturally. Without this union with God—this supernatural ingrafting in the Vine—there can be no fruit. If we do not abide in Him, we shall bear no fruit, we shall be cast forth, we shall wither in complete sterility. It is of paramount importance to remember this in our work as confessors.

Kindness in our treatment must be seconded by kindness in our judgment. Our primary duty in the confessional is to reconcile sinners with God. To do that we have to take cognizance of their offences. Now a man is guilty before God for the sin as he saw it himself, not as it is described in the text books or as it appears to the calm, considered judgment of a theologian. True, we have a duty of instruction where there is error. But even with an instructed penitent, one must always keep in mind the effect of a vague outlook, rather hard to define, that is shared with and borrowed from one's neighbours. It is best described as a weakened sense of sin. Theoretically one knows this action is sinful, a serious sin, still, in the decision to perform the action, one's views are unconsciously affected by the current outlook of one's fellows. "People, good people, do this; it can't be *so* bad." We do not intend to approve of this attitude; it is of course to be deplored. But it is there; and it may give the confessor an excuse—or rather a reason—for being lenient and indulgent in his judgment of the subjective guilt of the penitent. Readers of Canon Keatinge will remember how he insisted on confessors going to the classical authors for theological principles, but to the most recent and most lenient writers for their application, and how he qualified even those applications by the lack of this sense of sin, nowadays so widespread, which should make such a great difference in the outlook of the confessor to-day as compared with that of the confessor of fifty years ago. The point can only be hinted at here. It is mentioned merely to indicate how a confessor can, and we think should, modify the more harsh judgment of earlier writers whose days were passed in places and times in which the sense of the malice of sin was strong and effective. We repeat, the confessor has to deal with the sinner's offence as the sinner sees it. Anything that interferes with his judgment, interferes with his responsibility. It is of course true that one has to try to restore that sense of sin. Sometime perhaps where the lack of it is peculiar to an individual, drastic tactics may succeed—although we personally would not like to take the responsibility of using them. In the long run, they give the penitent a wrong concept of Christ's loving mercy. But where the outlook is widespread, such a policy is fatal and really unjustified. The point is that a priest is a bridge or—if you prefer it—a bridge-builder. He has to mediate between God and men. He has to reconcile this man to God. He gets God's teaching from his theological training, but he has to be prepared to enter into the views of this particular individual sinner. He cannot merely dogmatize in a general way, blandly—or angrily, perhaps—indifferent to the special views and difficulties of this particular penitent. He must use sympathy and understanding, tact and kindness. He

cannot expect the penitent to see his sins as a trained theologian sees them when in the austere calm of his study. The
penitent lives in a world of passion and prejudice, of thought-
lessness and activity. He is surrounded by incitements to
passion and to sin. He is carried away by the rush of
circumstances, the tempo of the times, the shrieking shallow-
ness of modern thought. Granted that one must help him
to overcome all that, yet one must remember all that is there
to be overcome. It cannot be ignored or harshly rejected.

It is by their failure to make some attempt at seeing the
penitent's point of view that so many confessors give the
impression that the Church is unreasonable in her demands,
that her burdens are unbearable. Our Lord's yoke is easy
and His burden light. We blaspheme Him by making it
otherwise. Two things are necessary to avoid these faults.
One is an understanding of our penitent's outlook and
circumstances, or at least, a realization that we do not
understand and a readiness to make allowances for the
effects of the un-understood factor. The other is a wider
reading of moral theology than a single text book affords.
Nowhere is the "man of one book" so dangerous to souls
as in the confessional.

How often do we meet a priest telling us: "But the book
says—*semper est grave.*" The book! No one author can be
dogmatic about anything but principles. Men differ and
their circumstances differ; and these differences often mean
that the results of the application of theological principles
to particular cases will be different. At least, if we are
probabilists, we should give the penitent the benefit of
authors' differences. One book cannot enable us to do that.
It is essential that a confessor should bear in mind the
different views of some representative authors on current
matters of conscience. It is further necessary that he take
into consideration the considerable changes that have taken
place in customs and, as a consequence, in the normal
reactions of human emotions to incitement. We think, too,
that confessors should realize the widespread occurrence of
nervous conditions—neuroses of various types—which may
sufficiently interfere with the psychological factors necessary
for grave subjective sin. This is highly important in dealing
with habitual sinners. In fact, it is a point for the discussion

of which a whole book would be necessary. However, to show how extensive the effects of such conditions can be, let us quote the words of the General Secretary of the Liverpool Area of the Discharged Prisoners' Association: "80 per cent. of men and women sentenced to terms of imprisonment to-day are not completely responsible for their anti-social activities by reason of varying degrees of mental deficiency. The other 20 per cent alone can be justly accused of sin and crime," (cf. Eng. Cath. Times: 29 Aug, 1947).

We have wandered somewhat outside the scope of this book which is concerned with the priest's spiritual life rather than his professional activity. But we have felt it necessary to discuss this particular phase of his professional work, lest a sensitive conscience might dictate unnecessary strictness or rigour in the confessional.

One other point is essential. There must be no professional jealousy or rivalry in regard to penitents. Deliberately to seek popularity or personal success is dastardly in a confessor, for it interferes immediately with his freedom of action and judgment in the sacred tribunal. Some priests, despite intense spirituality, will have to bear the cross of lack of popularity as a confessor—often through no fault of their own. By accepting this cross as Christ accepted His they can achieve untold fruit in souls. Some one else may reap the harvest—they however have done the sowing of it. But these are exceptions. A deeply spiritual man will nearly always be a successful confessor—for one cannot be truly spiritual unless one abides in the Vine which is Christ; and that is the principle of success.

HUMILITY

THE POWERS bestowed on every priest at ordination are beyond all calculation. The Holy Ghost Himself is there given to us, together with an official claim upon His adequate assistance in every work of our ministry. This claim is based not upon our own personal merit but upon the needs of the moment. It is not destroyed by any weight of personal sin, for it is backed by the merits of Christ. What is it then that so limits the harvest ? Why are we so often powerless to convert souls. ? How is it that we have not already achieved the wonders commensurate with our divine equipment ?

One might reply by citing the example of Our Lord Himself, Whose labours among the Jews were so obstructed by the hardness of their hearts and by their lack of faith. Yet the application of the time-tried principle: "Blame yourself first!" will lead us to the discovery of a still greater obstacle to our success. This is the want of humility. Let it be said quite bluntly, that, in practice, both for our own sanctification and that of the souls in our charge, nothing is so essential for us priests as true humility. It may even be said that if we have humility we have all that is necessary, for all else will be added on to us. And if we have not humility, all else profits us nothing. These are strong statements; but they find their justification in the words of the Scripture teaching us that *God resists the proud and gives grace to the humble*, (cf. James, iv. 6). To appreciate properly the importance and the function of humility, we must recall God's purpose in creating the world. He created it and planned it and saved it and rules it and acts on it and in it, for His own glory. And that glory is His own. He will not give it to another. He is the Lord God!

And, in this life at least, it is by His mercy that He intends to be glorified. The glory of His justice belongs rather to the next life. Now, mercy is the generosity of goodness when confronted with misery. If we do not know and acknowledge our own misery, we cannot know and glorify the mercy of God. Humility is a glad recognition of one's misery and of God's mercy. To it God gives grace, for we have our

Divine Master's assurance that this poverty is our title to
His mercy: *Blessed are the poor in spirit for theirs is the Kingdom
of Heaven.* The whole secret of the spiritual life is summed up
in that promise. For us priests it is of vital importance that
we understand this plan of Divine action, and that we live
by it and act by it. This is essentially true of our work in
the care of souls. In his ministry the work of the priest has
something of the note of *ex opere operato* about it. He acts
in persona Christi, (cf. Pius X, Letter to Priests, 1908). He is
another Christ. He has the merits of Christ and the power
of God at his disposal. He is working for the building up
of the Mystical Body of Christ, and God's paternal goodness
is always "in act"; so that the priest's own personal unworthiness or incompetence should not interfere with the
Divine action on souls in which he is merely an instrument.
But if he attributes it to his own cleverness, his own merit,
his own eloquence, then he prevents the fulfilment of the
Divine plan—for God resists him. God will not give His
glory to another. Indeed He cannot do so without self-
contradiction, for He is the Lord God.

Pride makes us appropriate to ourselves the glory of all
the good we have or we do, and is therefore directly opposed
to God's action. That is true of all our actions, but especially
true of apostolic work. For every single advance in the
supernatural life of any soul is the work of grace, and God
alone is the Author of grace. It was merited for souls by
Christ on the Cross. It is poured forth on souls by the Holy
Ghost, whose instruments we are. It is a superhuman work,
completely above our natural powers. To presume that our
cleverness in argument, our eloquence in preaching, our
kindness in receiving sinners, or learning, our zeal, our
personality, our prayers—our self, in fact—are anything but
instruments in the hands of God, when it is a question of
giving supernatural life or increasing it, is utter folly and
nonsense. That God designs to associate us with Himself in
His work is but the favour of His mercy. He has no need of
any of us; any need there is in the matter, is our need of Him.
If then by choosing us to be priests, He "lets us in on the
ground floor," so to speak, in His marvellous work of His
mercy, surely we have more reason than anyone else to realise
how gratuitous it is! What have we that we have not received?

Here again, St. Paul is our model: *Power is made perfect in infirmity. Gladly, therefore, will I glory in my infirmities, that the power of Christ may dwell in me,* (II Cor., xii: 9); *God forbid that I should glory, save in the cross of Our Lord Jesus Christ,* (Gal., vi: 14).

If we priests could only realise something of the infinite Fatherliness of God, of His natural urge to communicate Himself to souls—for *bonum est sui diffusivum,* and He is *Bonum Infinitum;* if we could only realise something of the infinite merits of Christ which are communicated to each soul at Baptism as if that soul itself had suffered and died as Our Lord did, (cf. St. Thomas, 3, 69, 2); if we could only remember that we are the instruments of Infinite Love, Who is the Holy Ghost,—there would be no limit to the confidence with which we approach our work for souls. Our own weakness would only be a new motive for confidence, for the weaker we are, the less likely is our co-operation in the work to take away from God's glory. And this glory is the motive of all His action! St. Paul sums it all up for us: *For see your vocation, brethren . . . the foolish things of the world hath God chosen that He may confound the wise; the weak things of the world hath God chosen, that He may confound the strong. And the base things of the world, and the things that are contemptible, hath God chosen and the things that are not, that He might bring to naught the things that are: that no flesh should glory in His sight. But of Him are you in Christ Jesus, Who of God is made unto us wisdom, and justice, and sanctification, and redemption; that as it is written, He that glorieth, may glory in the Lord,* (I Cor. i. 26-31).

The need for humility also becomes evident from another point of view. Our own personal attitude to God, as we have seen in previous chapters, is expressed by offering sacrifice. By sacrifice we profess and acknowledge God's sovereign dominion over us, and our complete dependence upon Him. This, of course, would be true of any sacrifice. But the sacrifice we offer is the sacrifice of Christ, sacramentally renewed in the Mass. In doing so, we identify ourselves with Christ in His death—are we not baptised into His death?—and His death is but the complete sacrificial summing up of His whole life. To identify ourselves with Him in our life, we must be like Him *meek and humble of heart,* we must empty ourself, for He emptied Himself . . . *becoming obedient unto death, even to the death of the Cross.*

There is no better way of rendering God the worship we owe Him as creatures, of fulfilling the assertion we make to Him by sacrifice, of conforming ourselves to the image of His Son Whose sacrifice we offer as our own, than by the practice of humility. It is the true interior sacrifice of praise; it alone gives God due honour and glory. For pride attributes to ourself all the good we do or have; humility attributes all to God. Humility alone can truly say to God: *Thine O Lord is magnificence, and power, and glory and victory: and to Thee is praise*, (I Par. xxix. 11).

This continual willingness to refer all we have or do to God links up our humility with our Mass, and with God's First Commandment. Reverence, according to St. Thomas, is the root of humility: *Principium et radix humilitatis est reverentia quam quis habet ad Deum. Humilitas causatur ex reverentia divina . . . Humilitas proprie respicit reverentiam qua homo Deo subjicitur*, (2, 2: 161; 1, 4, 5, 6). And this is but an echo of the foundation of St. Benedict's spiritual teaching. We tend to overlook the duty of direct devotion to God and His Glory. This duty is best fulfilled by humility, for such an habitual attitude of our soul can make our whole life a continual sacrifice of praise.

True humility is always accompanied by boundless confidence. Pride sees in our own self with its apparent excellence, our claim on God's co-operation, and on God's rewards; but even pride must admit that the very basis of such a claim sets a limit to it. Humility bases its confidence on personal poverty of spirit, and on the infinite mercy of God; it takes its stand on the merits of Christ, knowing that then nothing will be wanting to us in any grace. The Queen of Prophets has foretold it all to us. *Dispersit superbos mente cordis sui . . . exaltavit humiles Esurientes implevit bonis, divites dimisit inanes*, (Luke. ii, 51-53). Let us repeat it again: *Deus superbis resistit; humilibus autem dat gratiam.*

If humility, then, is so important for our service of God, for our sanctification, and for the salvation of others, how are we to acquire it? How are we to practise it? The full answer to that would require a complete treatise on the spiritual life—for the perfection of humility, in practice, coincides with the perfection of holiness. As a starting point, the obvious thing is to learn humility from our Divine Master and Model. We must develop our knowledge of Him by reading, by reflection, and by personal contact in prayer. It is impossible to be His friend, to talk to Him daily with any degree of sincerity, and not grow in humility.

Then, we must ask for the grace of humility in sincere and earnest prayer, basing our requests on the merits of Christ, and His zeal for the glory of God. To petition we should add prayerful consideration of the nature of God and His perfections. In fact, the rational basis for humility can be found in the tracts *De Deo Uno* and *De Deo Creatore et Conservatore*. Even the metaphysics of first and second causes can be of great help to the philosophically-minded. Therein one sees that it is not mere sentimental piety that talks of our "complete dependence of God in all we are or have or do."

In addition, we must try to accept humiliations when they come to us, and to be determined in checking the conscious manifestations of pride. Self-exaltation, even in our thoughts, must be avoided; so, also, must all referring, in thought, or word, of our success, to our own excellence or skill. That does not mean that we have to deny the good or talents that are in us. Quite the contrary—for humility is truth. But while recognising our assets, we must remember that they are only on loan. They came from God and they are for God.

The Magnificat is full of lessons in true humility. Our Lady knew that She was the most wonderful work of God's hands apart from the human nature of His Son. Yet She was the humblest of God's creatures. She knew and admitted that it was God Who made Her great—and that it was in His mercy that He did so. It is God also Who can make us truly humble. It would seem that the higher degrees of humility are the result of a special grace; prayer, then, is the way to obtain the perfection of humility, but our prayer is not sincere if we do not at the same time make a very reasonable effort to combat our own pride and prepare the soil of our soul for the Divine sowing.

It is not easy to come to an end when treating of humility. Much must be left unsaid in a short chapter. But one hint cannot be omitted. Competition is nearly always the work of pride; so also is every search for something to distinguish us from our fellows or to set us above them. Even mortification, even holiness, can be pursued through pride. We must be continually on our guard and constant in our prayer against illusions. The peace and confidence of the truly humble man are beyond all telling. He need no more be afraid of the "other fellow's" success; he need never again fear to admit his own failings; he need never again be restless and anxious about his own dignity and value. His hope and help is in the name of the Lord—which is "Saviour." His confidence is based on his own misery and God's mercy. His union with God is the fruit of his own nothingness and his own need. Gladly does he glory in his infirmities that the power of Christ may dwell in him. Again we may repeat it: *Humilibus autem Deus dat gratiam.*

OUR DAILY TIME-TABLE

BEFORE WE CONSIDER the question of the personal devotion to Our Lord and to His Mother which should be the foundation of a priest's spiritual life, we feel bound to point out the great need that each priest has for some rule of life. If the planning of our day is left to the caprice of the moment it is likely that we shall be like fallen leaves at the mercy of every little breeze of momentary interest or passing whim, circling around in some corner, getting nowhere. Even though we be men with a strong sense of duty, determined to overcome our caprices and to live each day in accordance with our ideals, yet, faced with an almost unbroken series of decisions to be made, we shall either waste all our energy in making these decisions instead of in carrying them out, or else we shall fail to decide and shall never succeed in devoting all our energies to any one particular task. There are so many duties crying out for attention, that any one of them can only be done properly by deciding to close our ears to the claims of the others. Our very sense of duty and the urgency of our many obligations may even paralyse our power of decision and inhibit or sadly mar our power of acting. One cannot pray if one feels one should really be visiting the sick, and one cannot give one's whole attention to a caller if one is listening to the clamour of the unprepared sermon. It is true that it would be impossible to draw up in advance a complete plan for each day; some things depend completely on circumstances. Yet there are a number of decisions that can and should be made once and for all, and there are many things which will not be done if some regular time is not set apart for doing them.

On the other hand, there is a tremendous help to be got from routine. Every man who has marched in step with his fellowmen knows how the steady swing of the group can carry a man on, far beyond the limits of his normal powers. Even when walking alone, a constant, regular pace can lend a man extra strength and extra endurance, whereas, if we have to break step or to change rhythm too frequently, we are soon fatigued. It is the starting and the stopping that use up power. The same principle must be applied to our life

H   111

as priests. We can easily see for ourselves what a wonderful asset a regular habit of doing things can be. Just think what it would mean in a few years if, for example, we read the Bible for even five minutes before dinner every day. And, to repeat, we may be quite certain that there are many things in a priest's life which, if they are not done by making them the object of a regular habit and routine, will never be done at all. There must, then, be some rule of life; that is beyond argument. It is quite another matter when we ask what that rule is to be. Here the present writer, a monk, is more than usually unfitted to prescribe. Yet there are some things upon which we may all argue and reach a working agreement. The first thing, to our mind, is to fix the hour of going to bed. Admittedly this may depend upon the time appointed for our morning Mass—which may be variable. Yet the time for going to bed should be fixed so as to give us say, seven hours of sleep. We say seven hours; but each man will have to decide for himself whether he needs more or less. If he needs more, let him be sure to see that he gets it by fixing a suitable time to retire. Otherwise he will find himself taking the necessary additional ration during his prayers or elsewhere when on duty. Then we have to fix the time for getting up. Promptness in rising at the appointed time is a most important mortification in the life of a priest. It can have far-reaching consequences. It is not altogether unconnected with our promptness in repelling temptations. A stolen few minutes more in bed may have to be paid for very dearly.

The hour of rising must be chosen so as to leave us sufficient time to be ready for Mass. What being ready for Mass means will depend to some extent upon personal outlook. It certainly means more than being washed, clothed, and shaved. Some prayer is essential. Here we are faced with the vexed question of where in our time-table we are going to put our mental prayer. Many authorities insist the mental prayer should be made in the morning before Mass. There are many advantages to be gained by following their advice and certainly their view cannot be set aside without good reason. But for our own part, we must admit that if a particular priest finds great difficulty in making his prayer in the morning and is able and willing to perform it in the evening, we would be prepared to sanction his proposal, if only for no other reason than that he is more likely to persevere in the practice under more congenial conditions. Men's mental habits differ. For some men, it will be certainly much easier to pray in the evening. In their case, however, we would strongly advise a short time of private prayer early in the morning before Mass, and we would insist upon some other form of prayer, either the Rosary or part of the Divine Office, for example, or else at least some spiritual reading. We take it for granted that the priest has anticipated Matins and Lauds; Prime then, at least, could be said before Mass. For the rest of the Office it is not easy to prescribe. But some special time should be set apart for Vespers and Compline, and also for Matins and Lauds.

So much depends upon a man's daily duties, that it is impossible to prescribe a detailed time-table. There is a great deal to be said for getting in some reading somewhere in the morning, if one's duties allow of it. In fact, for the man who makes his mental prayer in the evening, spiritual reading is necessary in the morning, if not before Mass, at least after breakfast. It will help him to supernaturalize his day; it will give him food for thought in his spare moments, and it will, generally speaking, orient his day towards God. Canon Keatinge in his excellent work *The Priest, His Character, and His Work,* makes a capital proposal to each priest. He asks him *to give God two hours before breakfast.* He visualizes those two hours in this way: the first for meditation and Mass, the second for thanksgiving and the Divine Office. Without insisting upon this particular arrangement, we would earnestly urge this proposal of two hours for God before breakfast, on all priests. Certainly a man who is faithful to such a practice will never go far wrong. Admittedly, it is a fairly high standard; but there is no room for mediocrity in the priesthood. Mediocrity is only the beginning of laxity and is, therefore, fatal for the priest. We must never forget what God told St. John to write to one of His priests: "Because thou art lukewarm and neither cold nor hot. . . . !" We know the rest. It is perhaps the most awful thing God ever said to man. The same Canon Keatinge asks for something more, and adding our plea to his we beg the priest to pass as much of those two hours as he can *in his church*. It is extraordinary how easy it is—and how common —for a priest to get out of the habit of using the church for his private devotions. The habit is well worth forming and following.

There is another point which we owe to Canon Keatinge. He suggests that the two hours after breakfast are "the hours most easily frittered away, if not entirely wasted." Experience will have taught most of us how true it is. There are, of course, many priests who find that these hours are full of work; but if we are not one of their number, it would be well to examine our conscience and ask ourselves what use we make of those hours after breakfast. The rest of the day must be planned in accordance with one's duties. If we stop to think of all the things that have to be fitted in to our time-table, we shall feel like a man whose room is littered with various articles—each essential—to be packed, and who is wondering how all that mighty multitude is to be fitted into one small valise. Yet luggage has been packed satisfactorily and successfully, and time-tables can be managed without any greater difficulty. Some experience by trial and error may be necessary before we achieve the right result.

The first difficulty of making a time-table having been overcome, the second difficulty—that of keeping to it—has to be faced. And in practice, one must at the same time face the third difficulty in this matter—that of departing from one's time-table. In regard to keeping to it, there are certain elements of it, especially those related to our spiritual exercises, about which we must be absolutely obstinate. There is no other word for it! Only obstinacy and grim determination will keep a man to the daily practice of prayer and of spiritual reading; and the chaff and banter, and the not-impossible ridicule of our clerical brethren, will soon make us depart from many other points of our plan, if we are not doggedly—aye, mulishly, obstinate. Yet combined with that obstinacy, there must be prudence and liberty of spirit. There are demands of duty—sudden sick-calls—and claims of charity against which no rule of life may be allowed to prevail. Obstinacy under such circumstances ceases to be a supernatural virtue and can easily become a natural vice.

Self-love refuses to alter its own plans for anyone else. Liberty of spirit is always ready for a departure from our rule in order to serve our neighbour, even if it may be to put up with an unwelcome visitor, for here we also give ourself to Christ in His members. All a priest's life consists in giving himself to God, either in direct service through Christ or else in indirect service to the members of Christ. This view of our ministry is most important. Impatience, touchiness, grumbling at the demands of our flock, are all quite incompatible with this devotion to the whole Christ. So also is self-will, even when it wants to carry out its own rule of life despite the lawful demand of Christ's members. Perhaps it would help if we said that our rule of life is a programme of the service of Christ, which may only be set aside to serve Christ in some other way, but which must always be set aside when Christ clearly asks us for service elsewhere.

To take but one example of the ambivalence that can be evident in this matter. Most priests will only persevere in clerical studies by fixing some time for that purpose and forcing themselves to keep to it. They will have to be quite obstinate about it. Yet there are men who can get so wrapped up in their studies that all interruptions are most distasteful and they get quite annoyed if anyone makes any claim—however just or urgent—on their services that would interfere with their work. Either way, there is need for obstinate devotion to Christ; both in perfecting oneself as His member in the priesthood and in serving our neighbour as a member of the Mystical Body. A priest must belong completely to Christ and be ready to give himself always.

Not only must our programme for the day be arranged, but also that for our week. There is a sermon to be prepared, possibly more than one. It is essential that some day be set apart for that, preferably early in the week. We are not here discussing how sermons should be prepared; our own views on that question are not quite conventional, but we all agree that they must be prepared somehow, and most of us know that that will not be done unless we have pre-arranged a day and a date for the purpose. Saturday is definitely *not* the day. And the priest who always preaches *extempore*, no matter how "successful," will have a lot to answer for. If he can preach a good sermon on the spur of the moment, he can preach a better one, and a much more effective one, after making some proper preparation. Such a methodical planning of our day and our week may seem burdensome. It might even seem to be harmful by repressing a certain spontaneous activity that can be so energetic. Yet appearances in that case are deceitful. "Spasmodic sprints" in a long-distance race will soon put an end to any hope of finishing the course in good time. The steady pace is what breaks the record. This is just as true of our clerical life. A priest has so many things to do that he could do none of them with the easy mind and the undivided attention that each of them needs if he had to be continually worrying about the others. The only way is to make our decision once and for all, giving all or each duty its due time, and then ceasing to worry about it. *Age quod agis!* This is true of mere natural efficiency. It is much more true of our supernatural life. It is difficult enough to devote all one's energies to any task and still be recollected in and with God; but it would be impossible to do so if we were needlessly uncertain as to what we really should be doing at this particular moment. A time-table properly arranged will facilitate not only our work but also our union with God— and this latter is the one and only principle of all supernatural fruitfulness.

PREACHING

THERE IS STILL one point in the priest's work which we must consider before going on to his interior life with Christ. It is his preaching. We are not here concerned with the technical aspect of preaching, but rather with its relations with a priest's spiritual life. Cardinal Manning in *The Eternal Priesthood* has a chapter on the subject well worth reading. There he indicates one most important point. Preparation is required for preaching, and the most important preparation is *not* the preparation of the sermon, but the preparation of the *man*. "The man (it is who) preaches, not the sermon, and the sermon is as the man is." And he adds another consideration that is as significant. Some men in preaching depend on their memory; either the memory of what they have written out, or else of what they have read and copied from others. The real preacher is one who *thinks*, and who speaks out of the fulness of his *present* consciousness. If we are remembering, we must stop thinking; if we are thinking, memory is suspended. If we are thinkers, we must think words, and words will come to express our thoughts. If our minds were full of the things of God and His Kingdom; if we realised them and lived in them as the conviction of our reason and the affection of our hearts, to speak of them would be a relief. And the Cardinal assures us: "it is the desire to be eloquent and to shine as orators that causes unreality, vain glory, and emptiness. If we could forget ourselves and speak seriously for God, we should find less difficulty in preaching, and the people would hear us gladly, because they would believe that we mean what we say. They are quick to perceive, it may be said, to feel, whether a priest speaks from his heart or only from his lips!" We should like to quote the Cardinal at length: space, however, is wanting. We can only appeal to each priest's own experience to confirm the truth of the Cardinal's observations. And once the truth is admitted, namely, that the preparation of the man is far more important than the preparation of the sermon, it will, we hope, become clear that none of the time which we have been asking the busy priest to devote to the exercises of the interior life is wasted, even from the point of view of his active ministry.

To avoid misunderstanding let it be clearly stated that we do not at all hold the opinion that sermons should not be prepared. Quite the contrary. No matter how well the man himself is prepared, he must be diligent in deciding how to express his message. He must choose his words, he must order his thoughts, he must review his texts. Whether that is to be done by writing out the whole sermon or not is another matter. Personally we would prefer to see the framework planned and then to have the preacher preach his sermon to himself, say, while going for a walk. In this way he can choose his words and censor his thoughts. Such a preparation does not take away the bloom of freshness or destroy the sincerity of spontaneous utterance which are so important in a sermon. However, all that is rather outside our present scope. The point is that the preacher needs to be a man of interior life, a spiritual man, one who has cultivated the interior virtues. And, further, he must be diligent in exercising these virtues, especially when in the pulpit. There must be a complete subordination of the natural to the supernatural, of ornament to function, of the man to Christ. Interior mortification and humility are essential. Pulpit oratory can easily be an empty art, a pagan vanity. It can please the ear without disturbing the conscience. It can stir up emotions without touching the will. Even at its best, it is merely natural; of itself, it can produce no supernatural effect. Is it too much to say that much of pulpit oratory can be a vice in a priest ?

It is true that reverence for God and for His service obliges us to do all things well. And in preaching, charity towards our congregation will lead us to make our sermon as attractive as possible. Yet we must never rely on any mere natural accomplishment to produce a supernatural effect. The turning of souls to God is the work of grace, and although we have the grace of state when preaching—a point no priest should ever forget—yet of all the graces, those *gratis datae* are the least susceptible of personal appropriation. They are lent to us by God, for the congregation, through the merits of some one else. It is sheer pride and robbery to claim them as our own—to put our own signature to the work a sermon accomplishes. And we know that God resists the proud. Humility in the preacher we repeat, is *essential*. In administering the Sacraments, no priest would be crazy enough to claim for himself the credit of the effect produced. Even though he absolves sin in the first person singular, he realizes that the power, the credit, and the glory belong unalienably to God. His own contribution is something that comes from his priesthood rather than from his own personal talent. The absolution of any other priest, duly appointed, would be equally efficacious. In preaching, however, the relative insignificance of the human contribution to the final result is by no means so obvious. In preaching there is certainly far more room for self-congratulation, for preening oneself in the rays of popular admiration, for putting one's own signature to the work of God's hands. This may be mere folly and thoughtless vanity; even so, it is bad enough; but if it be true pride, then it is fatal, for it is written "God *resists* the proud."

Humility, however, draws down grace, and the humble preacher, conscious and patient of his shortcomings, can always rely on God to come to his aid, not indeed to make him famous, but to convert souls by his own infirmities. "*To the humble, God giveth grace.*" Internal mortification is necessary. There are men who enjoy saying a thing well so much that one can almost hear them rolling the words around in their mouth and savouring them. There are men who are so full of themselves that they preach themselves, not Christ. There are men who have pet hobbies and will preach nothing else. There are men who will do all they can to avoid preaching unless the circumstances are such that they will shine. Preaching, like politics, is very often the science of the second-best. For a man will often have to treat a subject which is uncongenial, under conditions which handicap him, without the time for proper preparation. Then he must glory in his infirmities, especially when they are made manifest.

Self-denial, in a very literal sense, is another essential virtue for the preacher. He must be careful that neither he nor his sermon comes between his hearers and the end to which he would lead them. He must build a bridge between men and God—not a barrier. All his art, all his

talents, his oratory, his style, his learning, must be unobtrusive and completely subordinated to the purpose of the
sermon—which is to preach Christ. A priest in the pulpit
should always strive to follow Our Lord's example by
putting himself completely in the hands of the Holy Spirit.
To do that, he may often have to sacrifice very much that is
dear to him: self-satisfaction, natural "success," his reputation
and renown; but this is his vocation. He is a *priest;* and the
office of priest implies sacrifice. Our Lord Himself warns us
that self-denial must be characteristic of His disciples.
The interior life of the priest, so necessary for fruitful action,
will manifest itself in his sermons by a certain simplicity
and sincerity. It is true that there are occasions which call
for a more elaborate eloquence than usual; but even then,
the sermon should be born rather of the occasion than of the
personal prowess of the preacher. The effect of this genuine
spirituality may be noticed in another way also—in the
sincere sympathy which adapts itself readily to the different
varieties of human temperament to whom a priest must
preach. True charity will adapt the sermon to the needs
of the congregation without any of that patronizing con-
descension that sometimes marks the efforts of a speaker to
come down to the level of his audience, or of that obvious
obsequiousness which lay orators sometimes employ to
flatter their listeners.

In another way, too, union with God will affect the sermon. It is true a preacher may have to rebuke and to con-
demn sin; even Our Lord Himself denounced the Pharisees
very directly and very drastically. Would it be too much to
suggest that there are too many priests who seem to model
the style of all their sermons on that one particular example?
One wonders what fruit they reap. Certainly, there is
danger that they may do more harm than good. Denounce
sin—by all means–but as to the sinner—well, it is written:
"*This man receiveth sinners.*" It is a peculiar thing about
holiness, that it begets and displays a wonderful sympathy
for sinners. It is almost, as it were, a case of extremes
meeting. The holier a priest is, the more a sinner feels at
his ease with him. One might almost speak of a "fellow
feeling." Certainly, sympathy for sinners, even for great
sinners, should be characteristic of Christian preaching.

Much more could be written on this subject, but it lies on the border of our purpose in these chapters, which is rather the personal spirituality of the priest, and we have gone to our limits. The just man lives by faith. So also, the Christ-preacher preaches by faith. He believes in the Holy Spirit and in the action of His grace on the souls of the hearers. It is curious that it is often the least important, and the least satisfactory part of the sermon that actually brings grace to souls. Ultimately we must rely on the grace of our priesthood. It will work, not so much by giving us eloquence, as by giving our hearers illumination. Let us serve God by trying to preach in a manner worthy of Him, but let us serve souls, by relying more on God's grace than on our own eloquence to bring them to God.

STUDIES

IN A FORMER CHAPTER, we pointed out that there were some things which a priest certainly ought to do, but which he probably would not do unless he fixed a time for them in a planned programme. One of the most outstanding of these is clerical study. Even though in these chapters we are primarily concerned with the spiritual life, yet we cannot omit a discussion of the duty of study, on account of its manifold relations with both the priest's apostolate and his own spiritual advancement. It may seem unreasonable and impractical to suggest that a busy priest should, or even can, set aside a regular period for study. His day is already overfull and there are many other things still clamouring to be done. Nevertheless we insist that there is a duty incumbent on every priest to study and that this duty is an urgent one, and in some ways especially urgent for the priest who is too busy to study. First of all let us listen to the late Holy Father Pius XI. In his Encyclical on the Priesthood (1935) he insists : "The priest should have a full grasp of the Catholic teaching on faith and morals; he should know how to present it to others, and he should be able to give the reasons for the dogmas, laws, and observances of the Church of which he is a minister. . . Therefore, it is necessary that the priest, even among the absorbing tasks of his charge, and even with a view to it, should continue his theological studies with unremitting zeal. The knowledge acquired in the seminary is indeed a sufficient foundation with which to begin; but it must be grasped more thoroughly, and perfectly by an ever-increasing knowledge and understanding of the sacred sciences. *Herein is the source of effective preaching and of influence over the souls of others.*" These are weighty words. They come from the Vicar of Christ. They are not mere rhetoric. They must be taken literally. They are an apt commentary on Canon 129 of the Code. No priest dare set them aside as inapplicable to *his* particular case.

It is true that there are certain examinations that have to be faced. One must prepare for them. The less said about preparing for examinations the better. It is generally mere seasonal cramming, leaving little permanent residue. It leaves us far from the "thorough grasp . . . the ever-increasing knowledge and understanding," of which the Pope speaks. It is true that most of us read some reviews, but how many priests have ever even re-read the seminary course in dogma and moral after ordination ? How often does it happen that, when a priest is asked a question on moral theology, he glibly answers, as the only opinion, what he was taught in the seminary, blandly and unjustly excluding another probable view, which would often make a great difference to some of his penitents ? There is no science where the man of one book is such a public danger as in moral theology. Every priest has to hear confessions. He has no right to deprive his penitents of the liberty that comes from lack of certain agreement among theologians. And even if one book were enough, no man can understand one book, or realise all the implications of an unobtrusive adjective or qualifying phrase, if he has read no other book on the same subject. Theological principles are standard. But in the application of them, each theologian, however shrewd, is liable to be influenced by the particular type of persons and circumstances of which he has experience. An Italian theologian writing in Naples would probably have views of the excitability of human nature quite different from those of a Swedish theologian living near the Arctic circle. If that is kept in mind, the need for a second author in moral theology may be more evident. Even in dogma, despite its serene remoteness from the varieties of human temperament, a second author can be almost a revelation. One will suddenly realise that there are difficulties in the question which our seminary author never dealt with. New arguments, new points of view, new light, are the result of going to another author. Even apart from the benefit of plurality, there is the undeniable fact that no man can start "digesting" his four years' course in theology until he has been over it. It is only then that he can begin to understand the synthesis, to see things as a whole. And until he sees things as a whole, he cannot be a theologian.

To brush up, to review, to digest, and to expand our theological learning would seem work enough. But the Holy Father is not satisfied with that. He continues:

"Yet more is required. The dignity of the office he holds, and the maintenance of a becoming respect and esteem among the people, demand more than purely ecclesiastical learning. The priest must be graced by no less knowledge and culture than is usual among well-bred and well-educated people of his day. This is to say that he must be healthily modern. ..." Then the Holy Father encourages those whose tastes and special gifts draw them to specialise in a particular branch of science or art. He tells them that "they do not thereby deny their clerical profession," and he continues, "Among the rest of the clergy, none should remain content with a standard of learning or culture which sufficed, perhaps, in other times; they must try to attain—or, rather, they must actually attain—a higher standard of general education and of learning. It must be broader and more complete; and it must correspond to the generally higher level and wider scope of modern education as compared with the past."

And lest someone should cite the Curé of Ars and say that holiness is enough, he explains that Our Lord chose the saintly Curé so "that all might learn, if there be a choice, to prize holiness more than learning; not to place more trust in human than in divine means." But it is merely a question of perspective, for he adds: "In the natural order, divine miracles suspend for a moment the effect of physical laws, but do not revoke them. So, too, the case of these Saints, real living miracles in whom high sanctity made up for all the rest, does not make the lesson we have been teaching any the less true or necessary." Thus the Holy Father. And so if the Reverend Reader is a "real living miracle in whom high sanctity makes up for all the rest"—what we have to say about study does not apply to *him;* but if he is not quite so holy as all that, the obligation to study remains for him as laid down by Canon Law and by the Holy Father, Pius XI.

Many priests will wonder what "higher study" has got to do with their ministry to their particular parochial congregation. Common sense and experience tell them that their sermons and instructions must be as simple as possible. The finer points of thought or of style would be worse than useless in their pulpits. But even where their congregations are just ordinary, one must remember that it is the reserve of strength that gives force to the blow. The presentation of a simple outline of the faith demands wide knowledge and understanding of it. Even when talking to the *rudes*, our training and reading will—if properly used—be an asset to us. But there are few parishes where there are not at least some men of intelligence, some people who read, some people who think. Wherever men congregate, religious topics sooner or later come up for discussion, and the Catholic is often presented with many definite difficulties and problems. If his parish priest is not a man of learning to whom is he to go for help? Priests would often be very disturbed, when they have parried a few awkward questions from young people because of their inability to answer them and their unwillingness to admit it, if they could realise how clearly the young mind sees through them and how often the feeling is born in that mind that, after all, the Church is not quite all she says she is—the pillar and the ground of truth. A man of learning is always ready to admit the limits of his own knowledge. The man who is less wise does not even know his limitations. Such a man can do much damage to souls. His enquirers frequently see through his attempts to bluff them and may sometimes jump to a general conclusion of ecclesiastical ignorance from a particular example. All will readily admit the difficulty in dealing with questions that require abstract philosophy or wisdom of experience in the enquirer to make it possible for him to comprehend their solution. Yet bluffing or evasion is not the way to meet the difficulty. Far better—and more truly humble—to make a candid avowal of the position without attempting to be "patronising," and then, perhaps, to suggest some reading which would help the enquirer, if not to solve his problem, at least to understand how much is involved in its solution. But there are many difficulties which every priest should be able to handle, and no priest has a right to assume that there is no one in his parish who requires a solution for them. The thinking men are, of course, a small minority. Yet they cannot be overlooked. It is they who affect current thought and mould society. No priest dare confine his attention to the average middle of his parish. He must be prepared to deal with both extremes, even if it be only to send them to a specialist.

In his efforts to equip himself, a priest must not be

satisfied with mere knowledge as such. Understanding is also required. Nowadays it is fairly easy to acquire a superficial acquaintance with the more obvious facts in many branches of knowledge; and—if one may judge from the popularity of digests—there is a keen appetite for such information. Such knowledge is not enough for a priest and it would be fatal for him to think so. He must read and reflect enough to make him keep his head above the flood of facts that is so common nowadays. It may horrify the reader when we suggest that a return to philosophy is one way of avoiding that danger. Yet we would urge the priest not to overlook that branch of study, even if only to approach it through Ethics or Natural Theology, in both of which subjects some very fine books have recently appeared. However, that is rather a personal suggestion. *Qui potest capere—capiat.*

One reason why theological study is so important for the priest, is because dogma is the only proper foundation for devotion. Without it we are mere sentimentalists, or even emotionalists. Our separated brethren supply many illustrations of what spirituality without dogma can become. The subject is too big to treat of here; we content ourselves with assuring the priest that any time given to the study and understanding of dogma will pay very rich dividends in his spiritual life, to say nothing of its effects in his preaching and direction to others. But let us leave these sanctions and fall back upon the instructions of the Holy Father. These make it clear that it is the Will of God that a priest should study. He cannot then be true to his daily oblation of himself to God at Mass if he refuses to fulfil that obligation. This may seem a burden, but in reality it is a relief. For it means that no matter what opportunities of doing good a priest may have to pass over in order to comply with the law of the Church and the instructions of the Holy Father, he need not worry. He is doing something better. He is doing God's Will, and if his dispositions are right, by doing that he is in union with Christ—much more so than if he were engaged at any other task, however holy or apostolic. And union with Christ is the only way to bear fruit for God.

It is of utmost importance for every priest to realise this. And, as we say, it should be also a tremendous relief. Because, when a priest sits down to study, no matter how acutely he feels the call of souls in distress, he can assure himself that he is doing the very best thing that he can do to help them. That is one reason why we are so insistent on appealing to the Holy Father's instructions in this matter. They assure the priest that is God's Will for him. Doing God's Will is the surest way to divine union—in fact, given the right dispositions, it may be said to be divine union. And no one who remembers Our Lord's address to His Apostles at the Last Supper can deny that divine union is the way par excellence to bear fruit for souls and for God. No priest then, however busy he may be, need have any hesitation about setting some time apart for study. For some men, such work is congenial; but for many it can be rather tedious. The latter must remember that a priest is a man who has dedicated himself and his life completely to God, not merely when he undertook the office of the priesthood, but also each time he offers sacrifice to God. God has a right to determine how He shall be served. (That is the basis of our rejection of all forms of non-Catholic worship). And when He has indicated how He wishes a priest to serve Him, it would be a very false zeal which would induce a man to set aside God's wishes on the ground that he could serve Him better elsewhere.

UNION WITH JESUS

THERE IS ONE characteristic common to all the Saints and holy people of the Church—a characteristic that predominates in the lives of the Apostles. It is their personal love of Our Lord. By limiting his union to certain texts, a priest can consider his life as one of a labourer in God's vineyard winning souls by personal toil and effort, for the sake of an eternal reward. The dominant characteristic in such a conception is that of *service*. Now, this is quite different from Our Lord's view, as expressed when He said to His Apostles: *"You are My friends . . . I will not now call you servants."* And He went further, He insisted that they are the friends of His choice. *"I have chosen you,"* (Cf. John xv, 14-16). It is essential to remember this fact. We priests are chosen by Our Lord for a purpose. And the reason He chose us is not because of our own merits or talents, but because of His own goodness and mercy. He chose us because He loved us—loved us quite beyond our own merits. In fact, any good there is in us is because of His love for us. And having loved us, He has shared with us *everything*. He has made us part of Himself—sharers in His Priesthood. We share in His merits, in His powers, in His virtues; everything He has is at our own disposal. All is ours. He Himself is ours, for He dwells in our souls to share our lives. No amount of service, service as such, can return such love. If we want to realise how inadequate mere service would be, let us look around at the married couples we know, and note how dissatisfied a man or woman is who loves his or her consort intensely and receives in return only service—no matter how efficient that service may be. Personal love is essential in such cases. This is even more true of our case in regard to Our Lord. We must give Him personal love. One has only to read any of the literature in regard to the Sacred Heart to realise how much our personal love means to Our Lord and how little anything else of ours counts in His eyes if we do not give it to Him out of love.

Our Lord's plan for each priest is personal partnership: "We: Jesus and I." This is how He would have each priest live and act—in the first personal plural. Our Lord wants to share every moment of our life, especially every moment of our ministry. He wants us to live and work in complete dependence upon Himself and His love, never forgetting, never doubting it. He wants us to think of Him always in the second person singular—not the third, as many priests do. He wants us to be His friend; but He wants even more than that. He wants us to find in Him, and to give to Him, all the love that human hearts can give each other. Writing for English-speaking priests, one must here advert to the hesitation or reserve that some temperaments experience when there is talk of love—especially of love viewed from the more human side. Too-literal translations from the Romance languages, too emotional appeals addressed to us in our youth, too "precious" exhortations from some over-zealous nuns, exaggerated sentiment and pathos in sermons, bad art in poetry and painting, and a hundred and one other exaggerations of piety, may have "conditioned" us so that we are allergic to any appeal that even faintly recalls our past memories. Present-day psychology, too, has created in many minds a distrust of the more human side of devotion, though it is rather with reference to Our Lady than to Our Lord that it is operative. This is a spectre that must be laid. There are modern psychologists who seem to consider that all our motives and our attachments originate in some form of sex appetite. The higher movements of our heart are but sublimated "sex-drives," they hold. Even if that were true of the natural loves, we are here dealing with the supernatural.

But it is not even true of the natural. Even if we limit ourselves to the observations on which these writers base their conclusions, the most that can be suggested is that there is a fundamental, undifferentiated "drive" which can be turned towards various ends and utilized by various appetites. Working in countries where moral standards are lax, where there is little or no restraint on passion, and where children are often brought up without religion, it is not surprising that they should frequently find this "drive" has been associated with the strongest animal passion in man. But that does not mean that it originates in it. In fact, if one studied their material closely, I think one could find evidence in favour of the independent origin of these

I*

things. No one, especially a Catholic confessor, will question the frequency of their association and their significance. But a Catholic will also realise that all human relationships have their origin in the mind of the Creator and that, like the colours of the rainbow coming from white light, they are different components and manifestations of a higher love which contains them all eminently. It is much more scientific and much more certain to say that the love of a father, the love of a mother, the love of a brother, the love of a husband, the love of a friend, all manifest different aspects of a love that can be found burning in the Heart of Jesus—than to see in all these loves the mere "sublimation" of an animal passion in which they have their origin.

While all spiritual authorities agree that the natural can intrude and infect our motives in the spiritual life, I think we can safely set aside any fears based on the ideas of some modern psychologists about their fundamental origin. The love of God in our hearts is something supernatural, something poured out there by the Holy Spirit. All we have to do is to make our natural appetites subject to His sway, and we need have no hesitation in fulfilling the Divine commandment to love the Lord with our whole heart and our whole soul, with all our mind and all our strength. It is because this personal love of Our Lord is so important in the spiritual life of a priest, that we advert to these difficulties, which to many minds may seem merely chimerical. But one must try to meet the needs of all temperaments. Many are afraid of falling into sentimental excesses in their devotion if they give free rein to the heart in loving Our Lord. It might be well if they would consider for a moment the possibility of erring more seriously by being too cautious. We cannot get rid of human nature and its needs. As someone put it, translating the Latin tag: "You may drive nature out with a pitch fork, but it will always come home to roost." If one leaves the natural appetites of the heart starved by confining oneself to a too-abstract devotion, completely neglecting the claims of the flesh and blood, first of all one is depriving oneself of the great help which the emotions can be in the spiritual life when they are properly controlled; secondly, there is the danger that our hearts may seek their natural satisfaction in far more dangerous ways. It is not good for man to be alone; and if Jesus be not our friend, we may seek friendship—sentimental friendship—elsewhere and with disastrous results.

Then, too, there is the possibility that, by making God as remote as the Alpine snows, our service of Him may degenerate into something animated by a mere motive of gain that is quite close to selfishness. There are men who work—and work earnestly—from an abstract sense of duty and a sort of self-righteousness, sometimes achieving a sense of self-exaltation, giving thanks that they are not like the rest of men and, by ascribing to their own talents and diligence in the work of the ministry the success they achieve, thereby make themselves hateful in the eyes of God by their pride. External regularity and internal diligence are often more the work of self-love than of divine love. Such men rather repel souls than attract them. At least, when souls do come to them, they miss something, something which the close friend of Jesus is always able to give them, though often he is quite unconscious of the fact. If one is going to err, better to err on the side of forging too many bonds with Jesus, than too few. Our Lord wants all we have to give Him. If there is anything amiss in the manner of our giving He can rectify it. Let us then keep close to Him. How then are we to do this?

The first step is to ask help of Him who promised that we shall receive if we ask. And if our prayer is to be sincere we must be prepared to set aside all obstacles to companionship with Jesus. War has to be declared on habitual sin. Prejudices, inhibitions, reserves, have to be examined and deprived of any undue influence on our attitude. And then we must cultivate liberty of spirit. This is of the *utmost* importance. Companionship with Christ is not in practice a matter of physical nearness, for He is near us—He is in us—all the time. It rather depends on our avoidance of all things that would make us unwilling to advert to His presence. Now if we are over-scrupulous—if we are liable to see sin where there is really no sin—we shall be finding obstacles to this companionship all day long, and it will be unbearable. At the risk of differing from the views of many readers, we would suggest that the spiritual life—at least, in so far as companionship with Jesus is concerned—is far better served by a broad, wide, common-sense code of conduct, than a narrow, over-strict, rigorism that feels always bound to choose the better and the safer of two views. The point is that the liberal view leaves us free to share more of our life with Christ; and the more we keep in contact with Him, the better we shall become. The strict attitude—at first sight the safe one—only tends to make us turn away from Christ— and that is spiritual suicide.

The next step is to glory in our infirmities and to realise that the particular "formality" under which Christ unites Himself to us, is as our *Saviour*. He expects to find us infirm. He even expects to find that we are sinners. Even our sins need not separate us from Him, for He came to save sinners. If we offer them to Him and point out to Him that they are only symptoms of a more fundamental weakness and illness in our souls, we can forge a link with Him that need never embarrass us. For no patient is embarrassed by his illness in the presence of the doctor, and can one, even in one's wildest nightmares, imagine the Gentle Physician deserting a patient because he is ill ? No, the real trouble is that we are too proud to be merely His patients. We have not the humility, we have not the attitude of true spiritual childhood. *"Unless you be converted and become as little children you shall not enter the Kingdom of Heaven,"* (cf. Matt. xviii, 3). We do not know ourselves, because we do not want to know how weak we are, and we do not know the Heart of Jesus, because His goodness and mercy are well nigh unbelievable.

Perhaps the best way to indicate here how Our Lord wants to be regarded, is to quote from the notes of Sr. Josefa Menendez, passages which she records as having been uttered to her by Our Lord Himself. Without passing any judgment on their authenticity, no one who knows the doctrine of the Church can question their correspondence with actual reality. Sr. Josefa quotes Our Lord as saying: "Of consecrated priests and religious, My elect and chosen ones, I ask once more all their love, and that they should never, never, doubt Mine, and, above all, that they should trust Me implicitly. What is easier than reliance on My Heart . . . ? I shall make people understand that My first work in their souls has no other foundation than their own nothingness and frailty; and there begins the first link of the chain of love, which I prepare for them from all eternity. I ask for nothing better than to absolve erring souls . . . How tenderly I welcome those who after a first fall come to Me for pardon . . . and should they sin again, nay even often, I will forgive them a million, million times; love never wearies—and I will wash them in My Blood and blot out every stain from first to last. I do not want their union with Me to be of an indefinite character, but as close and intimate as that between two people who live in familiar friendship and who, even when no word is spoken, yet have a constant regard and mutual attention for one another—the result of their affection." These are but a few sentences from a collection of many such, but they should answer any objection one may feel to aspiring to close and constant companionship with one's Saviour.

Perhaps there is one mistake that may be responsible for our hesitation. Even though we regard Him as our Saviour, we think of His saving action as something confined to the past; He saved us from our past sins; but now that He has restored us to life, we feel that we cannot count in the same way on His saving grace if we fall again. That view is quite inadequate and incorrect. Our Lord is present to us every moment of our lives, saving us from ourselves, from the world, and from the devil. He is incessantly supplying for us, repairing our mistakes, supplying for our short-comings, supplementing us in every possible way. He will forgive us and restore us seventy times seven times. He is always Our Saviour, Our Jesus. Perhaps one more quotation from Sr. Josefa will help: "My love for them goes further: not only shall I make use of their daily life by giving their least actions a divine value, but I will make use of their very failings and frailties, and even their falls for the salvation of the world."

To them that love God, all things work together for good. No matter what we have done, or what we are, we can find in Jesus a Saviour Who, being omnipotent, is able to save us from everything and Whose Heart is burning with the desire to do so. We have only to go with confidence to the throne of grace. This life of companionship with Christ, sums up all that we have written about the spiritual life of the priest. If one lives and works in Christ's company, there is no need to worry about the different details of the spiritual life. They almost automatically look after themselves. The different virtues come into play as required, the various duties and exercises follow from our conversation with Christ. The little duties of the day take on a new significance. Companionship with Jesus sums up everything and vivifies everything. Did He not Himself sum it all up: "Abide in Me"? To find this companionship, to achieve it, to persevere in it, what are we to do? The answer can be given in one word. That word is "Mary." Where else shall we find the child, as Pius X asks, but in the arms of His Mother? Who else will unite us to Christ but she of whom the same Pope has written: "There is no one more capable of joining us with Christ," (*Ad diem illum*). Devotion to Mary then is an integral part of devotion to Christ and we shall consider it in our next chapter.

BEHOLD THY MOTHER

THE ASSOCIATION BETWEEN Mary and the priesthood dates back to its very institution. Christ Himself became our Priest in His Mother's womb at the moment when She was dedicating Herself to be the Mother of the Redeemer. When the same High Priest was sacrificing Himself on the Cross, His dying words announced Mary's maternal office in the Church and were addressed to the newly ordained St. John who "took her for his own." When the Holy Ghost came upon the infant Church at Pentecost we know that Mary was there, and here by Her prayers and example already began Her motherly charge of the Mystical Body of Christ.

The Biblical references to Mary though few are full of significance. In the very first book of Genesis we find the promise of our redemption pronounced in the unexpected form of a triumphant warfare between Mary and Satan, between Her Seed and his. And this very same plan appears again in the final book of the divine revelation when St. John tells us in the Apocalypse of the woman clothed with the sun, crowned with twelve stars and the moon at her feet. He sees Her as a mother giving life to a child, whom the dragon is waiting to devour. The importance and significance of this particular presentation of God's plan by the Holy Spirit must not be overlooked by us priests who are called to work in the very task of giving life to the Mystical Body of Christ and protecting it from the attacks of Satan. *No priest can do without Mary.* In Her merciful goodness She often co-operates without waiting for us to turn to Her, but deliberately to neglect Mary is to reduce our power of action on souls to a minimum if not to frustrate it completely.

The doctrine of the universal mediation of Mary is, of course, not a defined dogma. Yet it is so true and so certain that no priest can afford to overlook the fact that every grace of which he is the minister, is due, after Christ, to Mary. And in view of God's evident plan to associate Mary with Him in the triumph of the Redemption, is it too much to say that there are probably many graces that will not be given if Mary is not asked for them ? For it seems to be God's plan not only that we should obtain all things through Mary, but that we should recognize Her intervention so that She may have Her share of the glory.

The question of the exact part played by Our Lady in the work of Redemption and its application to the souls of men is a matter of controversy. But it is receiving more and more attention daily in the Church, and despite all the differences of opinion, there seems to be a steady tide of increasing support for the views which give Her a more prominent place in the scheme of things. Undoubtedly some enthusiasts exaggerate Her role, while others reduce it too much. In many countries where there is a large Protestant population, zeal for their conversion makes men anxious lest they should scandalize the weak. Despite all that, Her role as the New Eve in union with the New Adam is being examined and its details are being worked out, so that more and more She takes the place beside Her Son that it appears to be His Will to give Her. It is especially true that the present age is the age of Mary. Her action is becoming more evident and more extensive every day. Fatima is but one of many symptoms that draw attention to Her. She is the Mother of the Whole Christ; we priests have to share in that office. God having decided that the regeneration of the human race should be the work of a New Eve as well as of a new Adam—one has only to read St. Irenaeus to find how old the tradition is— we priests, all due proportion being guarded, can no more do without Mary than we can do without Christ. True, our dependence on Him is *ex natura rei*, and our dependence on Mary is only because God has so willed it. Yet She must co-operate with our work or else it will be sheer sterility.

Readers will pardon this discussion of dogma, but we feel it essential to remind them that devotion to Mary has a deep theological foundation. Too often it is preached as a matter of sentiment, or perhaps as a matter of expediency. Properly understood, it is a matter of necessity, for Mary's place in God's plan is no mere ornamental one, but pertains to its very integrity. Does not Pius X write: *Nimium scilicet haec comprobatur ex dolenda eorum ratione, qui aut daemonis aestu aut falsis opinionibus, adiutricem Virginem praeterire se posse autumnant. Miseri atque infelices, praetexunt se Mariam negligere, honorem, ut Christo, habeant:"ignorant tamen non inverniri nisi cum Matre eius,"* (Encl. *Ad diem illud.* 1904). The whole of this

Encyclical should be familiar to every priest; it is our answer to any who feel that what we have written is too strong.

The point is that God intends to put the devil in his place. That is more effectively done by making him experience his defeat through a human creature, and a woman at that, than by Divine action alone. It is true that Mary cannot be numbered among the foolish things of this earth, or the weak. But we ourselves do definitely belong there. And our choice by God to assist in His work of regeneration and liberation is part of the same policy of showing His power, by using mere human instruments to triumph over the prince of darkness. We need not be surprised then, that Mary is to be found active wherever grace flows. After all, grace is the life of the soul. Is not Mary our Mother ? We priests, then, both in our own spiritual life and our pastoral work must give Mary Her due place. We must honour Her, and incidentally remind ourselves of our dependence upon Her, by certain devotions. We must depend on Her in our work. We must have absolute confidence in Her, and we must try to put souls in contact with Her.

Personal devotion to Mary is not such an easy matter to prescribe in detail. The perfect way of being devoted to Her is to follow Her one commandment "Whatsoever He shall say to you, do ye." It implies the whole of the Christian life. To our mind the fundamental thing is rather an attitude of mind than a programme of practices. Still, an attitude of mind calls for external expression, and in fact grows by such expression. So that we must pray to Mary. Had I been writing this some years ago, I should have put a choice of two prayers to Mary before the reader, either the Little Office or the Rosary. There are so many men who find the Rosary hard to say that I should have agreed readily to their saying the Little Office instead. However the insistence of authority on the Rosary, (cf. Can. 125) and Our Lady's own request at Fatima make me hesitate. If one can at all manage to say a Rosary every day, it should be done. However, prudence makes me add that there may be cases where a more limited plan will succeed better. At least, let us decide to say the complete Rosary—fifteen decades—once a week. That means a decade every morning, a decade every evening,

and an extra one fitted in somewhere, say either on Saturday
or Sunday. Many of those who find the five decades a
difficult task, a penance rather than a prayer, will be
probably sufficiently courageous to face a decade at a time.
After all it can be said anywhere—and one should not be
afraid to say it while walking or moving about. If the
continual repetition dulls the meaning of the words for us,
at least we can console ourselves that the words in which
God made His proposal to the chosen Mother of His Son—
have a meaning and a memory for Mary that is beyond
telling. Surely, She will delight in these words of ours
even if we do not savour them, and after all, it is *She* whom
we want to please.

Still, the Rosary for some men will always be a problem.
Distractions, routine, repetition, tend to make it a mere
mechanical lip-offering. Often a man comes to the end of
the fifth decade of the beads to find his mind has been miles
away all the time. Public recitation with others is often a
help. Moving about is sometimes a remedy. Distributing the
five decades over different parts of the day may also serve.
But however poor our performance, no priest should ever
be satisfied with less than the fifteen decades a week. It may
not suit us—but Our Lady wants it that way. She has a
Mother's right to Her own way. If that is not enough, the
Little Office in whole or in part, will suit those who need a
printed page to keep their thoughts from wandering. The
use of an English translation will help to give the psalms
sufficient novelty in comparison with the Latin Psalms of
the Breviary. Again this is a devotion which is better distributed over different parts of the day. One word of
warning should be added. If the recitation of the Little
Office tends to make us rush the Breviary or interfere with
our discharge of it in any way—the Little Office should be
omitted. First things first, commands before counsels.
Far better say the Breviary well, and omit the Little Office,
than "get in" both of them at the cost of devotion or reverence. We can always say the Breviary in union with Our
Lady. This is a devotion earnestly to be recommended.
We say the office in the name of the Church. Surely Mary
says it with us. Why not say it with Her? A small picture pro-
truding from our Breviary will help to keep Her in our minds.

There are many other devotional practices, but one should
avoid overloading one's programme with different exercises.
A few simple exercises to express and to nourish our attitude
are sufficient. For the point about devotion to Mary is this—
that it is really only part of devotion to Christ. In the first
place in honouring Mary we are only acting in partnership
with Christ Who lives in us. In the second place, in seeking
Her protection, it is the life of Christ within us that we are
committing to Her care. So, too, in the work of our apostolate,
we go to Mary that She may bring forth and nourish the life
of Christ in the souls of those in our charge. In reality
devotion to Mary and devotion to Her Son are not two
completely separate devotions but are rather two different
aspects and ways of devotion to Christ. Instead then of
multiplying practices, it is better to show our devotion to
Mary by our devotion to Her Son. By doing our pastoral
work in partnership or better still in union with Mary we
are giving Her due honour, we are offering Her another
chance of doing something for Her Son, we are ensuring
the fruitfulness of our Apostolate, and we are exercising
quite a number of virtues that are especially pleasing to God.
In fact all the virtues of spiritual childhood can be found in
devotion to Mary. And as Benedict XV reminded us, this
spiritual childhood is *essential* for our salvation. "Unless
you be converted, and become as little children, *you shall not*
enter the Kingdom of Heaven."

No priest need ever fear that in paying attention to Mary,
he is neglecting Her Son. In the first place, Mary never
retains anything for Herself; everything we give Her is given
immediately to Her Son. She is a perfect mediatrix. She
only intervenes to unite more closely—She only receives to
give more perfectly. Secondly, it is the unfailing experience
of all who have preached devotion to Our Lady in any
sincerity, that they are gently but inevitably lead to a new
height of devotion to Her Son. And then only do we discover
the meaning of devotion to the Holy Ghost. In fact Mary
introduces us into the life of the Trinity in accordance with
the prayer of Her Son at the Last Supper. Devotion to the
Father, to the Son, to the Holy Ghost, devotion to the
Human Nature of the Son, devotion to His Mystical Body
all grow out of devotion to Mary and are welded in a truly

wonderful manner into a unity that at first sight seems impossible. *Gustate et videte*. The real devotion to Our Lady, as we have said, is an attitude of heart and mind. The best expression of this is the total consecration of oneself to Mary, on the lines indicated by St. Grignion de Montfort. This is so important that we shall discuss it in the following chapter. Let us add one remark. Every thing Christ received from this world was received through Mary. He had no human father. All His Body and Blood were derived from Her. His Soul was, of course, directly created by God; but His Body was formed from Mary's flesh and blood without any other human co-operation. Even after His birth, the food on which His Body grew, was prepared by Mary. There is a parallel in the growth of the Mystical Body. In some way or other all its " increase " must come through Mary. It is by Mary that we are fashioned and formed so as to be suitable food for the Mystical Body of Christ. And it is only in close union with, and complete dependence upon Mary, that we priests can unite souls to Christ. Her co-operation is *essential* for all the work of our apostolate. Let us quote Pius X ; " There is no more certain and more efficacious way of uniting all to Christ than by Mary. . . . Clearly there is no other alternative for us than to receive Christ from the hands of Mary," (*Ad diem illum*). We must, then, give Her Her proper place in our spiritual life and in every act of our apostolate.

CONSECRATION TO OUR LADY

DEVOTION TO OUR LADY being so important for the priest, both for his own spiritual life and in his apostolic ministry, it is only right that we should examine the form of devotion which St. Louis Grignion de Montfort expounded in his *True Devotion to The Blessed Virgin,* and in *The Secret of Mary.* This is all the more necessary, as the English translations of these works savour of the time and the fashion belonging to the original, and may seem too "flowery" and fanciful for the modern reader in English. Whatever we may think about the style—there can be no question about either the sublimity or the soundness of the doctrine. One has only to read the Encyclical of Pius X, *Ad diem illum* (Feb. 1904), to see how closely the ideas of St. Louis are in harmony with those of the Vicar of Christ.

The devotion proposed by St. Grignion consists in making a complete consecration of one's entire self to Mary by a special act, which act is but the initiation of a life of complete dependence upon and dedication to Her. The purpose of this action is to belong more completely to Jesus Christ and to be more closely and more securely united to Him. In a word, its purpose is "to abide in Him" as He Himself prescribed for all His Apostles. What does this consecration entail? By it we give Mary all that we are, all that we have, and all that we ever may become or receive—in a word every thing of which we have any power to dispose. We first of all give Mary our body and its future to be used in Her service either in activity or in suffering as She desires. As a consequence, we accept all the dispositions of Providence in regard to health, strength, skill, sickness, life and death, from the very beginning of our life to its end. In addition we give Her complete power of disposal over all our worldly possessions, relying on Her maternal care to provide for us and using all that we have in Her services. But the gift of our body is only a prelude to the greater gift of our soul. All our faculties are placed at Mary's disposal for the service of Her Son (we repeat, there is no difference between Her service and that of Her Son—they are one "in Christ"). We employ them for Her—not for our own glory—and we commit the outcome of our efforts to Her protection, accepting external failure and success with prudent indifference. Our soul itself, with the Christ life that Baptism has implanted therein, we put into Her hands, relying on Her to ensure its sanctification, its perseverance, and its ultimate union with God in heaven. In particular we see all that happens to us from a supernatural standpoint, from which the soul appears more important than the body, and eternity more important than time.

The offering however goes further. Our prayers and the prayers that are said for us, even after death, are made over to Her to divert according to Her intentions. That does not mean that we are not to pray for particular intentions. There are many just reasons why we should do so; in fact such intentions are often obligatory. Even in the Canon of the Mass we should not be afraid to specify our particular commemorations; to do so is more in accordance with the mind of the Church. But all our prayers should be offered up with the implicit intention that Mary can also apply their purport and application as She will. We have every reason to trust Her administrative powers. The supernatural value of our works also are included in our offering. The satisfactory and impetratory value is Hers to use as She pleases; but we even give Her our merits in so far as it is possible to do so. Merit *de condigno* is of course inalienable, but merit *de congruo* may sometimes be transferable. We however make no reserves; the whole supernatural bank account is made over to Mary to draw on whenever and however She wills.

It is essential if we are to understand this devotion properly to understand that it is only a means to an end. St. Louis de Montfort suggests a formula of consecration. The true nature of this devotion is shown in the fact that the dedication part of the prayer commences with a renewal of our baptismal vows, a complete donation of ourself "*to Jesus Christ*, the Incarnate Wisdom, to carry our cross after Him, all the days of our life, and to be more faithful to Him than we have ever been before." It then immediately proceeds to address Our Lady. "In the presence of the whole heavenly court I choose Thee this day for my Mother and Mistress. I deliver and consecrate to Thee, as Thy slave, my body, my soul, my goods both interior and exterior, and even the value of all my good actions, past, present and future, leaving to Thee the entire and full right of disposing of me; and of all that belongs to me, without exception, according to Thy good pleasure, and to the greatest glory of God in time and eternity." The final paragraph of the prayer is significant. "O Faithful Virgin, make me in all things so perfect a disciple, imitator and slave of the Incarnate Wisdom, Jesus Christ Thy Son, that by thy intercession and by Thy example, I may attain to the fulness of His Age on earth and of His Glory in heaven Amen."

We stress the fact that the chief purpose of this complete consecration to Mary is to achieve our complete consecration to Christ. Many Catholics are still afraid of devotion to Our Lady. They are afraid of exaggeration, of mere sentimentality, of interference with the honour due to God. They even suggest that it is better to go direct to Christ. This is a complete mistake. St. Louis de Montfort's own comment is noteworthy. "Be on your guard against believing that it would be more perfect to go straight to Jesus, straight to God. If you do so, your work and your intention will be of but little value; while if you go to Him through Mary, they will be the work of Mary in you, and consequently will be exalted and eminently worthy of being offered to God." Mary is the Mother of Christ. No mother is so inhuman as to steal the food of her children. We and all that we do, are the food of Christ. But just as Christ's natural body was formed in Mary, by Mary, and with Mary, so His mystical body is also formed in Mary, by Mary and with Mary. That is the way He has chosen. We cannot improve upon His arrangements.

It must be remembered that this devotion is no passing act; it is a life-long policy, a habitual attitude of mind, a continued turning of the heart. It needs frequent renewal, but often a smile or an imperceptible glance towards Our Lady is all that is necessary. It is not something to be undertaken without consideration and examination. Readers who wish to examine it will find all they need in De Montfort's two little books. There is also an excellent summary in Tanquerey's *Spiritual Life* and the same author discusses the question again in his *Doctrine and Devotion*. The classical work on the subject is: Lhoumeau: *La Vie Spirituelle à l'école de Montfort.*

It is also important to note, that the devotion does not interfere with our direct approach to Jesus Christ. On the contrary, it facilitates it. Mary is not like a mother who refuses to let her children be the centre of attention. She only desires to "decrease" that He may increase. When we do go to Jesus, it is with a new confidence that She is with us, interceding for us, excusing us, making the way easy for us. After all, we have crucified Him, and even though He has forgiven us, we may find it hard to forgive ourselves. As a result, our approach to Him is hampered by a sense of our sins. The knowledge that Mary is always with us, that we belong to Her, that He sees in us one of Her children, is of inestimable aid in overcoming our diffidence. And in learning how to rely on Her to go to Christ, we are unconsciously learning how to rely on Christ to go to God. There is hardly any more valuable lesson.

There is another similar parallel that arises in devotion to Our Lady. The secret of true devotion to Her, if one may so phrase it, is to become the nothingness that separates Jesus from Mary. All that Mary does to us is done to Christ, all that Christ does to us is done to Mary, with Mary we serve Christ, with Christ we may say that we honour Mary. Our whole life is a continual interchange of love between Jesus and Mary in which we are but a willing instrument. Now this is a fine image of what our life should be in regard to the Three Persons of the Blessed Trinity. Our ultimate vocation is to share in some mysterious way in that Divine Family Life. That vocation begins here on earth. The easiest way to learn it and to accomplish it is by sharing in the "Family Life" of Jesus and Mary. It is not necessary to develop this point here. Let it suffice to say—that no approach to Mary is ever permitted to end with Her. She sees that all movements of our heart to Her lead us ultimately to the Blessed Trinity.

The more immediate results of this consecration to Mary—if it be made with sincerity and generosity—are manifold and marvellous. There arises almost at once an extraordinary sense of positive peace and unbounded confidence, which no amount of strain or worry or danger or temptation can lessen. We belong to Mary: She will look after us and She can look after us much better than we can ourselves. Our work is for Mary and Mary's Son; She will guide it, She will aid it, She will ensure its fruitfulness. No matter what help we need, no matter what special grace is required, we feel sure that Mary in Her all-powerful intercession will obtain it in so far as God's plan demands it. Those special helps, the happy coincidences, the unexpected meetings, the chance words, the fortunate ideas,—that play so great a part in the work of the apostolate, begin to multiply in a striking manner. Mary will not be outdone in generosity. If we have given all to Her, She will not fail us.

If the whole of perfection may be summed up in the love of God for His own sake and of our neighbour for God, it is not an exaggeration to say that there is hardly a better way of fulfilling this law of perfection than by this complete consecration to Mary. Not only is it a complete offering of all that we have to God, but it is the most effective way of serving our neighbour. Even with the best will in the world, and the most complete generosity, no human mind can know where one's forces are best employed in the service of God. Even with the limits of our work marked out for us by authority, there is always the problem of what is best to do, which is the best line of attack to follow up. But when all is given to Mary, She applies all the results of our efforts at that point of the front in the battle between Christ and anti-Christ where they will be of most value and effect. Even though the particular end we have in view may not be reached and our efforts, say, to convert some soul end in failure, Mary will apply the supernatural efficacy of our work elsewhere with the most fruitful results. Let us not forget the extraordinary role that is marked out for Her in this "enmity" by God Himself as recorded in the third chapter of Genesis.

In giving Mary the control of our life, our development and our work, we are only following the example set by Our Lord for the first thirty years of His Life. Let us never forget how *completely* subject He was to Mary from the first moment of the Incarnation—how completely dependent upon Her, how completely at Her disposal. He has given us an example, that as He has done so also may we do.

The fundamental principle of the whole Christian life is incorporation in Christ. Whatever Mary does to us is done to Christ, so that abandoning ourselves to Her Maternal care, we are only giving Her another chance to do something for Her beloved Son. In fact we are giving Her an opportunity that our Lord Himself could not give Her. For we are stained with sin; we are but human creatures. Is there not something extra in the virtue that would stoop to help us which is not present in Her direct service of Her Divine Son. In "mothering" us, Mary can show Her love for Christ in a way that was never possible in regard to His own human nature. Let us give Her this opportunity and wonders will result.

CHRIST IN US

IT IS SURPRISING how small a part is played in the spiritual life of us priests by that tremendous truth of the divine indwelling in our souls. We have all studied the Treatise on Grace: we preach on the Sacraments; we warn our congregations that sin is the death of the soul; but what idea have we of what really is involved in the soul's supernatural life? Perhaps many texts of Scripture—especially those of St. Paul—which would help us to realize something of the extraordinary nature of this life of the soul have ceased to strike us because of their familiarity. One question, then, might help to set us thinking. Our Lord Himself warned us that unless we eat of His Body and drink of His Blood, we shall not have life in us. If, then, the Body and Blood of Christ must be the Food of our soul, what must be its life? Theologically, perhaps, we would answer, "grace." But that one word has a depth of meaning that is only too often ignored. For when we talk of grace, we usually have in our minds the notion of created grace. But this is only the effect of something far more fundamental. For created grace implies uncreated grace. And uncreated grace is God Himself. When a soul then, is in the state of grace, when a soul is supernaturally alive, God is in that soul. Some of His activities there may be appropriated to particular Persons of the Blessed Trinity. We know that St. Paul speaks of charity being poured out in our hearts by the Holy Ghost, Who is given to us. The Holy Spirit is literally given to us in Baptism, in Confirmation and in Ordination—in fact in all the Sacraments. He dwells in our souls, giving them life, making them share in some way in His own divine nature, making us not only in name but in very truth, sons of God. Let us be quite clear about it. This presence of God in our souls is something apart—something quite different from the threefold presence of God in His creatures. There is, of course, room for theological discussion as to the metaphysics of this presence. That, however, does not prevent our stating definitely that the Three Persons of the Blessed Trinity are really, truly and substantially present in our soul. Leo XIII, in his Encyclical on the Holy Ghost writes: "God, by grace, resides in the just soul as in a temple, in a most intimate and peculiar manner. From this proceeds that union of affection by which the soul adheres most closely to God, more so than a friend is united to his most loving and devoted friend, and enjoys God in all fulness and sweetness. Now this wonderful union, which is properly called "indwelling," differing only in degree or state from that with which God beatifies the Saints in Heaven, although it is certainly produced by the presence of the whole Blessed Trinity—"We will come to him and make our abode with him"—nevertheless is attributed in a peculiar manner to the Holy Ghost." Perhaps it will be of help to quote a standard theologian's summing up of his discussion of the subject. Hervé, in his Treatise on Grace, writes: "God, according to the gift of sanctifying grace is present in the soul in a new and quite special way, not only in so far as He infuses and conserves in us the supernatural gifts which are participations of Himself as He is in Himself (*participationes Ipsius prout in se est*), but also in as much as He personally dwells in us, giving Himself to us as something intimate and knowable *quasi experimentaliter*, which we can even now to some extent use and enjoy," (Hervé, Manual. Dogma. Vol. III, Par.54). Readers will forgive these quotations, but I would not dare suggest that we should "use" and "enjoy" God in our souls, without sound authority. The authority is quite sound, but what about our practice? Do we make use of God in our souls? Do we enjoy Him? Is there anybody who should do so as much as we priests should? We have received the Holy Ghost in ordination, and are made participators not merely in the nature, but in the priesthood of Christ. Our life is devoted to His work; it should be an intimate partnership with Him. Yet, too often it is something quite human and quite solitary. We do not remember—if we have ever really known—the Gift of God. For the Gift of God is God Himself.

One reason for this low level of living is that we adopt a wrong notion of what God wants. We think He wants service. We think He needs our co-operation in the salvation of souls. That of course is quite true—in one way. In another way, it is quite wrong. God certainly does not *need* our service, and He only wants it in so far as it comes from something else. For God wants our love and friendship. Nothing less will satisfy Him, nothing less will profit us in the slightest. God is in our souls to unite us intimately to Himself. He wants to vivify us with His grace, to give us the power to be His friends, to help us to love Him with a love that is the reflection of His own love for Himself. There is nothing wanting to us in any grace for we have in ourselves the Author of all grace—God Himself. He is ours! He is there to help us. He is our Paraclete. He is in our souls that we may have life and have it more abundantly. All we have to do is to let Him live His life in us, for us and for Himself.

That is just the trouble. We want to live for Him—but it is *our own* life that we intend to live. We tend to see in Him a source of the perfecting of *ourselves*, an ally in *our* schemes, a means to *our* ends. Now God is not in our souls to live our life, according to our views, however enlightened they may be. Our Lord has warned us with insistence that the spiritual life is a denial of ourselves. The Holy Ghost prompts St. Paul to picture it as a putting off of the old man and a putting on of something new, something fashioned in Christ, something animated and controlled by the Holy Spirit, something completely belonging to the Father—for we are His sons. It is almost a new creation. In a word, it is Christ. And Christ is All.

It is only when we ponder this great truth, when we read and re-read the Epistles of St. Paul and consider the calm statements of theologians that we begin to realise the amazing gulf that separates the Christian from the pagan, the supernatural from the natural, the divine from the human. And one is brought to wonder where among Catholics is to be seen the corresponding difference in the character and conduct of the men who have been raised to such a union with the divinity as have Catholics. And one may ask, in particular, why is there so much that is merely and entirely "natural" and just like the rest of men, even in us priests? One reason is that we do not take the spiritual life seriously enough. We have not a high enough idea of what we are, or that to which we are called. It is of the highest significance that that outstanding master of the spiritual life—St. Teresa of Avila—decided to portray it as a journey into a castle, through seven mansions; the goal of the journey is God

Himself, and the castle into which a man journeys in quest of God is his own soul. We look for God outside of ourselves, and all the time He is within. We try to find Him by our own efforts, and all the time, He is with us—is not His name Emmanuel?—waiting and wanting to be our help and strength. We set union with Him as the remote and distant object of our work, yet all the time union with Him is the beginning and the intimate source of all our activity. What, in practice, can we do about it? The first thing is to read a little book by Fr. de Jaegher, S.J., *One with Jesus*, to take our theology at its true value, to take St. Paul as truly inspired and to take God at His word. Then we have to devote ourselves to God within us. Now, this activity of God in our souls is attributed to the Holy Spirit, and we often find it hard to form an idea of the Holy Spirit that will seize our minds and animate our activity. But even in this matter Christ is our salvation. Jesus Christ is the revelation of God, and Christ Himself is present in us. Lest the theologians should raise their eyebrows, let me quote St. John Chrysostom: "*qui spiritum habet, non modo Christi esse dicitur, sed etiam ipsum habere Christum. Non potest enim, spiritu praesente, non adesse Christus. Ubi enim una Trinitas hypostasis adest, tota adest Trinitas,*" (In Ep. ad Rom. 13. 8).

Let us then take as our slogan the words of St. Paul, "*I live, now, not I, but Christ liveth in me,*" (Gal. ii. 20). Let us try to put this into practice. It means forgetting ourselves and remembering Christ. It means giving up our own petty narrow interests and assuming those of Christ. It means an end to "I": the pronoun now is always "we"—except when we say "peccavi." It means that when we pray, we let Christ pray in us, and second His prayer. It means that we are no longer put out or annoyed at the sight of our true selves, for we know that no matter what we are, Christ is saving us and supplying for us. It means that we give up the dream of making of ourselves and our lives something wonderful of our own creation, in which we can take pride; instead, we now leave it to Christ to communicate to us and to form in us a beauty that is a reflection of His own and that is of His making. It means complete abandonment to Christ, and complete self-surrender. There is one way of viewing the position that will help us to put this doctrine into practice and to make it a vital force in our lives. Let us realise that our life is a continuation of the life of Christ. The very words of St. John Chrysostom quoted above authorize us to say that it is the presence of God within us in a special manner, which makes our lives such a continuation. Fr. de Jaegher puts it very well in his little book *One with Jesus*. The finite life of Our Lord on earth, despite its infinite depth did not exhaust the love of Christ for His Father. He loved Him and devoted Himself to Him completely, for thirty-three years in complete subjection to the Holy Ghost. He wants to continue that life in each of us. For that purpose He comes into our soul with His Holy Spirit in Baptism. For that purpose He comes to us again and again and remains really, truly and substantially present in us as a Person, with the same Holy Spirit, every time we receive Holy Communion. We must never forget that even though the sacramental presence of His Body and Blood ceases when the sacred species are completely changed in our bodies, yet the divine Person of Our Saviour and His divinity remain in our soul, as long as we do not commit mortal sin. This personal presence is the end, the corporal presence is only a means to that end. Remaining then in us, burning with love for His Father and for us, He waits for the complete surrender of our heart and our will—of our whole self and our whole life. He wants to take over all our faculties that He may through them express His love of the Father in devoted service and submission to His will. Our hands, our lips, our minds and our hearts must be His. They are ours, and He will not take them by force; He waits for us to give them to Him. To give Him all he wants, all we have to do is to identify ourselves completely with Him. In every action, in every prayer, in every suffering, in every thought or act, we must decide that we are "Christ"—that He it is Who is acting, praying, suffering and living in us. Once we can reach this point of view and adopt it habitually there will come a wonderful transformation in our lives. For one thing, an entirely new meaning is given to our smallest actions. They now take their importance from our union with Christ, and this is what makes them fruitful. There is no longer any necessity to sigh for chances of "doing something" for God or for souls; there is no longer any reason

to be impatient with our personal limitations or with those
of our circumstances.   Our apostolic zeal—if it be truly
such—need not wait for "suitable" occasions of satisfying
itself. In all we say or do—if it is said or done in partnership
with Christ, and in subordination to Him—we abide in
Him, and by that very fact, bear much fruit. It is true, that
we may not have the earthly glory of it—but if that is what
we are seeking in our ministry, we are no longer true to our
vocation. The epitaph of those who thus "serve" God is
summary: "They have received their reward "

On the other hand, such a life of continual dependence on
God within us, opens the door to all the treasures of the
spiritual life. That region commonly called "mystical," and
so often and so wrongly regarded as something inaccessible,
something closed to "ordinary" souls, becomes opened up
for us, for the so-called mystical life is nothing but the full
development of the ordinary life of the Christian where the
Holy Ghost is allowed to have His way. This will be especially true of our prayer. When we go to pray we shall no
longer rely on our own efforts, but, just as in the Mass we
take over the Sacrifice of Christ, and making it ours, present
it to the Heavenly Father, so in prayer, we shall take over
the prayer of the Spirit of Christ, Who prayeth in us and
with us, as St. Paul and St. Patrick amply testify—and
making it our own, offer it up to the Father. This prayer
continues throughout the whole day. At any moment we
can turn to the Father saying: "Behold Thy well-beloved
Son in whom Thou art well-pleased. Hear Him !"—and
we have a perfect prayer of praise and thanksgiving of
atonement and intercession. Each need of the day, whether
it refers to ourselves or to those among whom we minister,
can find in this appeal a perfect manifestation to God,
which brings us absolute assurance of Heavenly aid. The
great difficulty is that we will not renounce ourselves. That
is probably partly due to the fact that we do not yet know
Our Lord sufficiently nor do we realise what He has done
for us, or what He has promised to do for us. He is our
Saviour. His Father is Our Father, His Spirit is our Sanctifier.
His life is full of hidden meanings and messages for those
who realise that our life is but a continuation of His. The
story of the Gospels takes on a new meaning when we re-read

it from this point of view. And the Mass takes on a new significance and importance for our personal spiritual life.

Many readers may feel that all this has nothing to do with themselves; they may see in what we have written a monastic ideal wrongly applied to the active life of the apostolate. The answer to that is found in the 14th Chapter of St. John. Our Lord was not talking to monks. He was talking to His Apostles, briefing them for their mission work, laying down the essential principles that must rule their life. These words of Our Lord are addressed to you, Father. You are a priest; you are an apostle; you are one of the Friends of Our Lord. He does not call you a servant. He has called you a friend, and insists that you must abide in Him and He in you. *Qui potest capere capiat.*

CHRIST IS ALL AND IN ALL

THE INCREASING PROMINENCE and importance given to the doctrine of the Mystical Body of Christ is one of the most significant features of the life of the Church in these days. But it is a doctrine which is far from easy to explain even where one has ample space, and adequate summarization is still more difficult. The Incarnation of the Son of God was the first part of God's plan to save men; the second part involves the union of all those who are to be saved in a supernatural organism, analogous to the organism of the human body, in which Christ is described as the Head, the Holy Spirit as the Soul, and each of us as the members. It is a unique union, and is therefore difficult to explain without error. Such errors have been made, and the present Holy Father has warned us against them. No matter how close or how intimate the union between the individual member and the Head may be, the human member never loses his own personality, nor is he dispensed from the need and obligation of making his own personal efforts, even though the fruit of his actions is due to the part played in them by Christ the Head of the Body.

The application of this doctrine, so rich and so many-sided, to the spiritual life presents many problems, so that if we confine ourselves here to one or two of the many possible points of view and merely try to suggest a few ways in which a priest can use them in his spiritual life, readers will, we hope, be patient, and will realize that no more can be attempted in a short article. But we can assure every reader that the doctrine, though difficult, is well worth exploring, and its study will lead to may new helps and hopes for our spiritual life. It is, however, not a doctrine of which the practical application can be summed up in a few lines. Through our membership of Christ we enter into new and marvellous relations with Christ and through Him with each Person of the Blessed Trinity. We have a new relationship to Mary, to the Saints, to the Souls in Purgatory, and very significantly to each of our fellow men. Even we are changed in ourselves, for St. Paul speaks of us as a "new creature" in Christ, (cf. ii Cor. v. 17). Some "remote" preparation, then, by way of reading and reflection is required on the part of each priest to enable him to apply the doctrine to his spiritual life.

A priest, for example, must be familiar with the doctrine of St. Paul, he should read some of the recent works on the Mystical Body, and he must try to form for himself some sort of a working notion of what is suggested by St. Paul's pregnant phrase "in Christ." He must try to realize that in all his contacts with his neighbour he himself is a member of the Body of Christ, and he is dealing with another member. Might it be suggested that instead of concentrating on the "pathology" of the members and their vices and sins, it would be well to give more attention to what may be termed the "physiology" of the Mystical Body—that is the normal inter-action of the members ?

In regard to the human body, physiologists discuss the workings of the heart, of the lungs, of the stomach, etc.; psychologists talk about the acts of the will, of the intellect, of the imagination; yet in both cases, one must always realize that the organ or the faculty is not really the agent. It is the human being who acts through the faculty or the organ, though in many such discussions this fact is over-looked. When we come to discuss the actions of the members of the Mystical Body of Christ, there are certain points of difference from the human organism that must not be forgotten. The members of the Mystical Body are persons, and they retain the dominion over their own actions. Yet even so, in their supernatural actions they do act alone. Each member has his own personal contribution to make, but that must not lead us to overlook the fact that God is also at work in a very special manner. The Spirit of Christ is the soul of our spiritual life, and even though a theological analysis of His action would be difficult, we can state that in all our supernatural actions Christ acts in us. Let us consider this for a moment.

Our Lord Himself taught His Apostles that He is the Vine, they the branches, and He warned them that they could only bear fruit by abiding in Him. If the branch is in the Vine, the Vine must be in the branch. If the branch bears fruit, can we deny that the Vine bears fruit ? Does not St. Paul exclaim: I live, now not I, but Christ liveth in me," (Gal. ii. 20)." Cajetan's commentary on this text authorizes our statement that Christ acts in us. "All my vital acts," he writes "such as to know, to think, to love, to be glad, or to be sad, to desire or to work, are mine no longer; they no longer come from me but from Christ within me." And when he discusses the merits of our good works, he writes: "The merit of eternal life is not attributed so much to our own works as to the works which, Christ our Head, performs in us and through us," (*De Fide et operibus*). This view was frequently repeated during the discussions at the Council of Trent. Let us admit that one must be careful to avoid the errors of pantheism or quietism in expressing it; but whatever about the formulation, the fact is that every time we priests perform a supernatural action, Christ is our partner, Christ is our Head, Christ is our Life; and we rob Him of His glory if we appropriate any of the good in our actions or in their fruits to ourselves.

That is the practical point. If we could only get out of the habit of patting ourselves on the back whenever we achieve something in God's service! When we consecrate or absolve, we know that through the sacrament of Order, Christ consecrates or absolves in us and by us. We forget that through Baptism and through the Blessed Eucharist Christ unites us to Himself and becomes the author of all our supernatural actions. The one word supernatural should remind us of the folly of any human agent claiming credit for a super-human work. True, God has attached merit to such works, but even such merit is the free gift of His mercy and the fruit of the merits of Christ. In fact it is only because of His mercy and love that He deigns to use us in His work. He allows us to contribute our tiny drop of water to the wine of His own work in order that we may have a title to merit. But we are worse than fools if we cannot overlook our own tiny contribution and try to remember Him who by His Passion and Death enables these things to be done and us to share in their doing.

If we could only remember that in all our contacts with souls, Christ is acting in us, and that we are acting on Christ, our whole outlook would be revolutionised. For we would immediately find a perfect basis for unlimited confidence, and a means of solving the very difficult problem of maintaining a spiritual life despite many activities. Consider first our ground for confidence. Whatever be our own sins, or the sins of our client, we are both members of Christ, and His merits are more than enough to wash away any obstacle to the gift of grace. It is of capital importance to remember this always. For the realization of the need for grace in dealing with souls may discourage us if we realise how unworthy we are because of our sins and negligences. Yet by Baptism Christ's merits are ours, as if we ourselves had suffered His Passion and Death. This is how St. Thomas puts it when discussing the effects of Baptism, (cf. Summa. iii. 69. 2). Through Christ and in Christ both of us, priest and client, have a claim—the claim of His well-Beloved Son in Whom He is well-pleased—on the aid of the Omnipotent Father. (Do we ever remember these words of the Creed?) Through Christ and in Christ we have the Holy Ghost Himself for our ally in changing human dispositions and rebellious wills. And if more be needed, as members of Christ we can appeal to Mary with extraordinary meaning and with unshakeable assurance: *Monstra te esse Matrem!*

If we could realize all this, there would be no limit to our confidence when faced with any problem in our apostolate— there would never be any need to try to deny our own limitations or any reason to let them discourage us. On the contrary, we should glory in them. They are the ground of our assurance and of confident courage, for like St. Paul, we glory in our own infirmities that the power of Christ may dwell in us. Like St. Paul, we say in all confidence: "For when I am weak, then am I powerful!" (ii Cor. xii. 10).

If a realization of the riches that are ours through our incorporation and function in the Mystical Body of Christ can lead to such unlimited confidence that we act, like Our Lord Himself, "as one having power," surely it is well worth going to the trouble of some difficult reading and reflection to build up that realisation. When we are suddenly faced with the problem of disposing some reluctant sinner in a busy confessional, there can be no question of pausing to make an explicit appeal to each member of the Blessed Trinity, as well as to the Woman God gave us to be our Mother. But, if by reading and thinking we have built up a sense of our relations with each Divine Person, there will be no need to formulate our thoughts explicitly when the

necessity for their aid arises; a silent appeal of our heart will
suffice to draw down Their mercy and Their assistance.
But such a silent appeal implies a deep appreciation of our
position, and this requires time and thought for its development.

Reading then is essential. No priest can afford to ignore
all that has been written recently on the Mystical Body.
Admittedly it means reading dogma; but why on earth
should a priest be afraid of dogma ? What else has he got to
build on? Readers who have access to the work of Fr. Mersch,
S.J., translated into English by Fr. Kelly, S.J. and published
by Bruce under the title, *The Whole Christ*, should consult
the chapter wherein he treats of St. Augustine's sermons to
the people. Nothing could be better calculated to startle
us into a true outlook on this wonderful doctrine. Consider
only two texts. Commenting the words of Our Lord: "For
them do I sanctify myself in truth," the Doctor of Grace
puts on the lips of Our Lord, the daring words: *"Quia et
ipsi sunt ego,"*—"For they too are Myself!" And he sums up
the whole aim and plan of the Redemption in a marvellous
phrase: *"Et erit unus Christus seipsum amans"*—"and there shall
be one Christ loving Himself."

If we only could get some idea of the extraordinary meaning underlying these two phrases, our studies would have an
amazing effect not only on our apostolate but on our whole
spiritual life. The great problem for the priest is to maintain
an interior life throughout all the exterior works of the
ministry. He is called to perfection, and yet the very life that
his vocation demands seems, at times, to be the greatest
obstacle to perfection. Yet the conflict cannot be more than
apparent. Since the vocation to holiness is there, so also must
the grace to achieve it. If a man realizes that in every contact
with souls he is acting in union with Christ in himself and
dealing with Christ in his neighbour, all his apostolic work
is a continual "sacrament" where he meets Our Lord, truly
present and attainable. If he realises that Our Lord sancti-
fied Himself for men, can he fail to see that he, too, must
sanctify himself, not merely for God's sake, but also for the
sake of the souls committed to his charge ? This, I think, is
where most priests tend to fail. They do not realize that
there is a connection between their own sanctification and

the welfare of the souls for whom they are responsible. If they could only realize this, it would mean an end to that impatient fretfulness that finds it hard to devote time so precious in the ministry to the work of maintaining and developing their own spiritual life.

This continual contact with Christ in oneself and in one's neighbour should be a source of great sanctification for the priest. In some ways, it is more efficacious than the contact we make with Him when we kneel before the Tabernacle. Every priest knows the awful sense of God's remoteness and impassibility that can strike us even when we hold the Host in our hands. We cannot "touch" Him. We can do nothing for Him. In souls, on the contrary, He is more at our mercy. Anything we can do for them, is done for and *to* Him. Such a view could be of great help to a priest in developing his spiritual life.

Despite its importance, we prefer not to try to develop this view here in any detail. For there is an individual approach in such matters which depends greatly on personal tastes, and the right outlook has to be discovered by each priest for himself. But the advantages of finding it are well worth the trouble involved. Consider how such an "integral" view of Christianity can affect our life. Instead of concentrating on our own "self," even though it be for the purpose of denying our self, we do what is infinitely better, for we concentrate on Christ, and thereby forget oneself and lose ourself in Him. We shall also be continually reminded of our need of Him and our union with Him.

Few men of our time have understood this spirituality so well as Dom Columba Marmion. It would be well worth while for every priest to read the life of that great Abbot, especially the chapters where his own inner life is laid bare, generally in his own words. Time and time again, we find him insisting that in all his works, he must imitate Our Lord who told us "My doctrine is not mine, but of Him that sent me"; he feels urged to lay down his whole personality before God so that Our Lord would have free disposal of all his actions, and would live and work in Him without hindrance. Like Our Lord, Dom Columba wanted to have everything from the Father. One could find in those notes of Dom Marmion which Dom Thibaut has summarized

for us in his work *Abbot Columba Marmion* (Sands) the source
of a spirituality which is eminently suitable for every diocesan
priest, and which, if adopted, would transform a priest's life
in a very short time. Its adequate exposition must wait for
a suitable opportunity, but we would here insist that
although Dom Marmion was a monk, his spiritual teaching
is, as Benedict XV told a Bishop, "the pure doctrine of the
Church,"—and one very eminently adapted to the life and
work of a diocesan priest; there is no question of its being
a spirituality reserved for the mystics or for the chosen few
for it is literally the birthright of every priest, being based
on our supernatural adoption as sons of God.

Unless a priest has grasped the temendous truth of our
supernatural adoption, unless he has some understanding
of our birthright as baptized souls, he will miss one of the
fundamental facts of Christianity, one which is of immense
importance for his own life and work. As we have said,
St. Thomas sums it up when he tells us that in Baptism
*"the Passion and Death of Christ are communicated as a remedy
to the baptized person as if he himself had suffered and died,"* (cf
iii, 69, a 2). And the Mass we offer, being as he
says "the perfect sacrament of the Passion," contains that
Passion and Death really, truly, and substantially, in a
sacramental form. Therefore the whole of Christ's merits
are *ours*, by our very baptism even, to offer to God every
morning in more than ample atonement and impetration
for the sins and needs of the whole world. No wonder St.
Paul urges us to glory in our infirmities, to go with confidence
to the throne of grace. There are no obstacles, except
deliberate pride on our part, which cannot be set aside
through the efficacy of such a sacrifice.

In Christ as His members we, as well as our neighbour, are
united to Him forming one mystical person with Him who
makes more than ample satisfaction and impetration for
our sins and needs. In Christ we, as well as our neighbour,
are loved by the Father for the sake of His well beloved Son,
to whom we are united. In Christ we can act "as one having
power" when dealing with souls. For the soul with whom we
deal is also a member of Christ and the whole power of God
is at our disposal for his sanctification if we but renounce
ourselves and put on Christ.

For this is the whole point. St. Augustine said "there shall be one Christ loving Himself." We love ourselves too much to let Christ love Himself in all our works. All that we do as priests, praying or preaching, at the altar or in the parish, should merely be the occasion of Christ loving Himself. It will be, if we forget ourselves, if we imitate Christ and live completely *ad Patrem*, entirely devoted to His Father's glory. For God made the world for His glory, and God acts on and in the world for His glory, and He will not and cannot give that glory to another. If when we use His power fruitfully, we claim the glory of it for ourselves, He must, by the very law of His nature, resist us. But if we are humble, if we give Him the glory, He will give us grace. There is a marvellous depth in Our Lord's warning that we can only be His disciples if we deny our self and follow Him. Doing that we shall see the fulfilment of St. Augustine's words: "There shall be one Christ loving Himself," since Christ it is Whom we must follow and must find, and through Him and with Him and in Him, in the unity of the Spirit is all the glory of God.